Punch Down Under

Designed by Bill Hewison
Edited by Susan Jeffreys

First impression October 1984
Second impression November 1984

FIRST PUBLISHED IN GREAT BRITAIN IN 1984 BY ROBSON BOOKS LTD., BOLSOVER HOUSE, 5-6 CLIPSTONE STREET, LONDON W1P 7EB.

British Library Cataloguing in Publication Data
Humphries, Barry
Punch Down Under.
1. Australia — Social life and customs — Anecdotes, facetiae, satire, etc.
I. Title
994.06'3'0207 DU107

ISBN 0 86051 296 7

Printed in Great Britain by
Redwood Burn Ltd, Trowbridge, Wiltshire and
bound by Pegasus Bookbinding, Melksham, Wiltshire

Punch Down Under

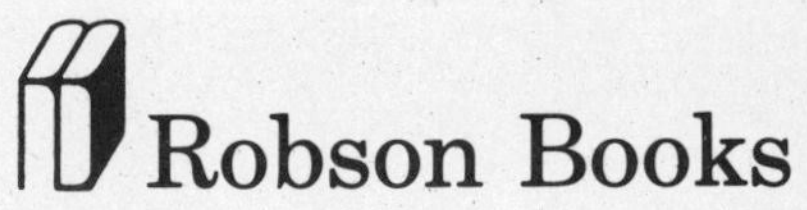

Robson Books

Contents

Introduction

It's the land of milk and honey,
It's so rich and safe and... funny.

Thus hymned a celebrated Australian diva in the Royal Albert Hall a few years ago. The country she extolled was, of course, her homeland, which has so prodigally enriched the musical stage of Europe, although never, in the view of several critics, so much as on that September evening in London.

As the huge British audience vented its hoarse hosannas and demanded a final glimpse of the *monstre sacre* from Melbourne, one felt that the singer's sentiments had touched a responsive, trans-hemispheric chord.

Australia is funny.

Indeed, *Punch* have thought so for over a hundred years, as this book testifies. Yet, strange to say, it is impossible to imagine such a volume devoted to the other Dominions. Wonderful, beaver-ridden, Mountie-infested Canada somehow fails to 'arouse the lions of laughter', and the boiling mud-pools of New Zealand, brushed by the ginger stubble of clustered kiwi-fruit, evoke powerful emotions, the least of which is mirth.

Australia has the advantage of *looking* funny.

In *Lady Windermere's Fan*, Wilde compared it to a large packing-case. It is both remote and prosaic, exotic and pedantic. It is Wembley in South-East Asia; a tropical Manchester. In recent times it has received massive injections of people from Greece, Jugoslavia, the Lebanon and Vietnam, all of whom will contrive, within one generation, to look Irish.

Less readily assimilated are Australia's native animals which upstage all-comers in the zoological Theatre of the Absurd. A country swarming with wombats, emus, quokkas, bandicoots, platypusses and numbats just *has* to be funnier than the tame European world of Beatrix Potter.

But in spite of such formidable competition from the indigenous wildlife, our best jokes remain anthropomorphic.

Australian politicians, for example, are a richly comic assembly of sanctimonious bores, rogues and roughnecks. Alas, they are largely immune to the purgative therapy of satire and criticism — except the most flaccid or modishly leftist — due to Australia's restrictive libel laws, surely the most stringent this side of the Iron Curtain.

Yet, though it has no Intelligentsia whatsoever, Australia produces an enormous number of artists; or people who would like to be artists. Most of these artists who do not pursue careers abroad, are ingenious mendicants, engaged in a ceaseless struggle to wrest alms from the gigantic bureaucracy which administers Australia's cultural life.

Until very recently, this bureaucracy was a strict custodian of the Official Australian Image: outdoor, sports-loving, clean-living. No matter that Sydney, for example, was fast becoming the shirt-lifters' and pillow-biters' capital of the world!

Many years ago I wrote, for one of *Punch*'s more strident competitors, a comic strip about a mythical Australian expatriate who incorporated some of my countrymen's seemingly irreconcilable qualities: bravery, incontinence, sentimentality, profanity, loyalty and latent satyriasis.

A film of the strip followed which was subsidised by the Government, though it seemed unlikely that anyone in Canberra had read the book or the screenplay, or, indeed, any screenplay or book. However, just as we were about to take off for our Earls Court location, a scrofulous Sydney civil servant from the Arts Council bounded across the tarmac and buttonholed the director.

'Excuse I, Bruce,' he panted, 'but I hope there won't be any *colloquialisms* in this fillum.'

Soon after, an international Australian airline and the purveyors of an emetic beer which I had once misguidedly 'put on the map', dissociated themselves from this (now classic) photoplay.

Comedy was fine, so long as it was not at the expense of Australia, and to suggest that the inhabitants of the sub-continent employed vernacular speech was deemed subversive to the national interest.

Like my comic strip hero, Barry Mackenzie, Australian officialdom cherished fantasies about 'niceness' and the womenfolk, and Gracious Living which seemed patently at odds with the realities of Australian social conduct.

Fifteen years later, the Authorities have performed a *volte face*, and the aforementioned airline and brewery now make television commercials in an arch, quasi-colloquial style, with much flaunting of humanely-culled marsupial fur, whilst the Australian Tourist Commission attempts to snare Americans with a scrubbed-up Mackenzie clone.

But new taboos have arisen. For example, women, lesbians and aborigines, or individuals in whom all three disadvantages are united, can no longer be laughed at in Australia. The Authorities and their watchdogs are constantly inventing new 'no go' areas upon which wags may trespass at their own considerable risk.

At the Opera House, Leeds, I recently impersonated a likeable Melbourne housewife who apostrophized her audience on various aspects of perception. The performance was interrupted by a noisy demo by the local chapter of Australian feminists protesting that my act 'degraded Australian women'. It is an ominous sign of the times that grim, boiler-suited vigilantes should be sent so far afield to police the image of Austral womanhood, and rebuke people like me who dare to portray my countrywomen as attractive, voluble, gladiolus-waving and tastefully frocked.

Perhaps, after all, it is wiser and safer to leave the task of laughing at Australia to the Poms. It is widely accepted that they are pathetically jealous of our steaks and sunshine, our sheilahs and our Brechtian puppet theatre. Indeed, is it not envy above all which permeates the following pages from the earliest anonymous *Punch* contributor, to the writings of that recent guest in Australia, Alan Coren; writings which give a new dimension to the epithet: English gratitude.

Whatever our shortcomings, I hope that we Australians can laugh at ourselves — it would be a sad old world if we could not. But there is one thing in this volume which is likely to cause serious offence to Australian readers, and that is the persistent depiction of my countrymen in hats with corks depending from the brim. I have never worn such a hat, and I have never met a man or woman who has. It is true that we have flies, and, moreover, it is true that we sometimes wear hats. It is the English who have added the corks. It is not dignified, and I am afraid it is *not funny*.

Auckland, July 1984 — Barry Humphries

"That's the Mackenzie spread—bloody hypochondriacs."

Australia — Land of the Rising Damp

HARRY SECOMBE

"Official opening today of a rain forest aviary at Taronga Zoo was washed out.

Minister for Lands, Mr Lewis, who was to perform the opening ceremony, went to a tailor to be fitted for a new suit."

Sydney Sun, December 16

WHETHER Mr Lewis went to his tailor in a fit of pique, or because he had nothing else to do, or whether he had gone along early to the aviary and had the suit he was wearing christened by the birds, is a matter for fascinating conjecture. However, my reason for including this cutting is to demonstrate to the folks at home the kind of summer we're having here in Sydney.

A commuter also wrote to a local paper complaining to the Suburban Railways Department that the carriages on the trains were leaking. A spokesman for the Department replied that they were aware that the carriages leaked, but it was only troublesome when it rained.

"Write something on how to live under that wretched sun," said the Editor when he discovered I was off to Australia. I nodded eagerly, my eyes already fixed on distant horizons, accepting the assignment in the spirit of a Stanley in search of an Antipodean Livingstone, my mind full of kangaroos, koalas and hot, burning beaches.

When I eventually landed at Sydney Airport, the sky was greyer than that over London when I left.

"You should have been here yesterday," said an airport official. "It was beaut."

At least I think that's what he said. I had caught a cold in Hong Kong, and apart from violent spasms of sneezing I also had a blockage in my left ear. (It cleared quite suddenly three days later when I hit a top note in "Bless This House" during a second-house performance in Adelaide—much to the surprise of the band who had finished playing and were on their way home.)

On arrival at my hotel in Kings

Cross the heavens opened, embracing me and my luggage. I entered the foyer with my tropical-weight suit plastered to my body and squelched my way to the Reception Desk.

"You're Harry Secombe," said a lady nearby.

I smiled, warmed by the recognition.

"Why aren't you taller?" she demanded rather crossly.

"Try adjusting your horizontal hold," I replied—cleverly, I thought—but she had gone.

In the lift the porter said, "Should have been here yesterday. It was beaut." He was on my good side at the time, so he definitely said it.

The sign on the landing outside my room said "To the Swimming Pool". I unpacked my luggage and sat on the bed in my bathing trunks waiting hopefully for the hot Australian sun to make an appearance. Four hours later I woke up shivering, my nose streaming with cold, and rain lashing the windows.

The house doctor was very sympathetic, "You've got a touch of the 'wog'," he said. "Better stay in bed tomorrow."

Of course, the sun came out in the morning, but all I got from it was sunburnt pyjamas.

The following day I felt better and was eager to sample the sunshine, but one look out of the window was enough. Rain and wind.

The commissionaire touched his cap as I stepped into the rainswept street.

"Shocking weather—you should have been here yesterday. It was beaut."

"I was," I said, splashing him playfully with drops from my bush hat.

Thus it has been since I arrived here. The warmth of Australian hospitality is tremendous; people have even loaned me their cars, something I've never known at home, and I've had so much free booze that my liver must resemble that of a Strasbourg goose. But nobody can turn on the sun. I spent a week in Adelaide, a lovely city with fine wide streets placed by its founder, Colonel William Light, on either side of the River Torrens, giving it a belt of parkland—a piece of town planning far ahead of its time. But I might just as well have been in Barnsley.

The cab driver from the airport had an answer for it. I opened the rear door of the taxi and got in.

"What's up, sport — have I got leprosy?"

I hurriedly got out again and sat beside him. We drove in silence through the rain until he said suddenly, "The weather's got into the wrong hands. They're manipulating it, mate."

I could only nod wordlessly, struck by the enormity of what "They" were doing.

When he dropped me off at the hotel he said, "Mind you, you should have been here yesterday."

"I know," I replied, "It was beaut."

"Nah," he said, "It was pissing down."

At Brisbane the temperature was ninety degrees, but still no sunshine. However, heartened by the weather forecast, I bought a pair of shorts and some long white stockings and set off for the cricket ground to watch the World Eleven play the first match against Australia. I sat with some friends in the Members' Pavilion, the only one in shorts, like some monstrous Boy Scout at a lone Jamboree. The temperature dropped about fifteen degrees in no time at all, and the effect on me was so great that at one period the umpires sent a message from the field to ask who was playing castanets in the pavilion. Later that afternoon a thunderstorm of frightening intensity stopped play and traffic in one fell swoop.

I began to think that the travel brochures would have to be rewritten. Or perhaps it was always like this, that the fabled Australian sunshine was indeed a fable—a product of the Tourist Board. Maybe the cab driver in Adelaide was right, "They" had somehow gained control of the weather. I went down with a bad cold again.

Back in Sydney I found that my old friend and fellow Army deserter Spike Milligan was in residence at Woy Woy, writing a sequel to his book book. I headed for Woy Woy on the next available train, to be hailed on my arrival at the station by a cry of "I'm over here, you bloody Welsh Zulu."

There stood my boon Goon companion hardly recognisable in a floppy hat, over-long trousers and a shirt which would have been too big on me.

The rest of the day I can only remember in kaleidoscope. I vaguely recall digging in his mother's garden for Blue Tongued Skink; a wild drive up a hillside in the pouring rain to look at a Red Gum Tree he was fond of; two bottles of beautiful Australian burgundy disappearing along with Mrs Milligan's curried chicken, and Spike deciding to start a Bell Bird sanctuary. This last decision resulted in a hilarious drive into the bush with a bewildered estate agent who was ordered to stop the car every few hundred yards while

Spike got out to listen for the call of the Bell Bird. He bought an acre of land to which I was witness, although it might have been the other way around. That night the rain didn't bother me at all.

The weather has its compensations, though. I have been able to while away the hours watching television, which is on four channels and starts at seven in the morning and finishes about one a.m. At present the programmes are on the summer schedules, a time when the top shows take a holiday and television becomes the Sargasso Sea of the cinema. All the films ever made seem to have drifted here and wallow sluggishly behind the screen. I swear I saw Finlay Currie as a young man one night last week—and even more appalling, I saw myself as a flickering fool in a film which I had fervently hoped had been cut up into celluloid collar stiffeners years ago. The last time I had heard of it, it was doing well in Afghanistan where, I believe, they are allowed to fire at the screen.

There is also a programme on the lines of Hughie Green's *Opportunity Knocks*, but with one big difference—the hopeful participant has to stand before the camera whilst a panel of professionals criticises his or her performance. It says much for the Australian temperament that since I have been watching the programme, no member of the panel has yet been physically attacked.

Wherever I have performed here I have met many "poms" who are always anxious to hear news from home. One gentleman with as strong a Welsh accent as ever I have heard came back-stage to see me.

"When did you leave home?" I asked, thinking he was fresh from the boat.

"Twenty years ago, boyo," he said.

It is very interesting to listen to the various accents here. Scottish, Irish and Welsh immigrants seem to retain their old way of speaking, and the stronger Northern dialects survive almost intact. On the other hand, I met a fellow I could have sworn was a "dinki-di" Australian, until after a few drinks he let slip the fact that he came from London only eight years ago, or whenever the Great Train Robbery was.

Tomorrow my family arrive from England and I shall be there at the airport to meet them. The weather forecast is "showers, heavy at times", so if it's raining when they arrive I've got my greeting ready.

"You should have been here yesterday. It was beaut."

The Neck Strine from Platform 2

PAUL JENNINGS

BETTER men than I have been fascinated by the idea of huge empty sunlit Australia (as unknown to the world until recently as his subconscious was to man) as a *symbolic* landscape— and I don't mean only painter S. Nolan. There was a review somewhere of *Voss*, by Patrick White (another great book I absolutely must read or I'll be seventy before I know where I am) lamenting the impossibility for an English novelist of making a journey inland from, say, Skegness (Lincs.) seem as symbolic as the great odyssey described in that universally praised Australian novel. And then there's the marvellous poem by D. H. Lawrence, about the kangaroo

She watches with insatiable wistfulness.
Untold centuries of watching for something to come,
For a new signal from life, in that silent lost land of the South
Where nothing bites but insects and snakes and the sun, small life,
Where no bull roared, no cow ever lowed, no stag cried, no leopard screeched, no lion coughed, no dog barked,
But all was silent save for parrots occasionally, in the haunted blue bush.
Wistfully watching, with wonderful liquid eyes.
And all her weight, all her blood, dripping sack-wise down towards the earth's centre...

It's impossible not to feel that the Australians, now they have come, are making up for lost time, their shouts echo across that huge continent; how like us, with their drinking hours and cricket and awful cooking, and the sacred "smoko," equivalent to our tea-break—and yet how unlike, in their relaxed openness!

Until I actually do read *Voss*, and probably even after, my chief imaginative short cut to the otherness of Australia is going to be the timetable of the Western Australian Government Railways. It's been on my desk for years because I seem to be using it as a file, and scarcely a day passes without a subliminal glance at some such place-name as Karrakatta or Cowcowing or Winceballup.

Don't misunderstand me. I know it's perfectly simple to look more closely and see that Karrakatta is thirteen minutes from Perth on the short suburban line to Fremantle, and is probably about as exotic as Notting Hill Gate. Yet even our station names do mysteriously tell you some basic truth about England, if you have ears to listen. Is there not something of Milton and Bunyan about that very Notting Hill Gate line, where you progress biblically through the *Marble Arch* to *Shepherd's Bush* and the ultimate shining *White City*? Does not the Piccadilly Line recall heraldic medieval and Shakespearean wars—*Baron's Court*, *Earl's Court*, *Gloucester Road*, *Knightsbridge*, *Leicester Square*, *King's Cross*?

But all this is buried under layers of old time and sooty brick. The point about my WA timetable is that here, for those of us who have never seen this dreamlike land and are likely to remain in our complex, subdivided, windswept, many roofed, art-groaning European towns for the rest of our lives, are names with a direct and sunlit freshness which must surely convey a poetically true vision of Australia.

The overwhelming impression is one of jovial sociability. Obviously the sight of a fellow human being at such places, nakedly functional in the vast emptiness, as *Toolibin*, *Thirty Mile Peg* or *Kronkup Turnoff* is one to quicken the heart, and perhaps to give rise to a long, semi-ritual conversation, a *Gabbin* or *Gabalong*. It would be nice to think that the Aborigines do this too, that whereas one goes "walkabout" on one's own, one goes *gabalong* with a companion.

This was the basic pioneering situation, but during the nineteenth century, as towns and settlements grew, this fundamental sociability found reflection in numerous social holidays which centred very much round the horse and horse-racing. Perhaps *Gwindinnup*, *Gwambygine*, *Jerramungup* and *Gidgieannup* were named after the actual cries with which the drivers of four-in-hands and buggies, streaming out in gay family parties to the races, urged on their horses.

The Irish, needles to say, were very prominent in all this. What should the racecourse itself be called but *Donnybrook*? And it is easy to imagine the colourful scene under that fluttering Victorian bunting, shining with the innocence of a primitive painting in a foreground of green grass, with distant views of eucalyptus and spinifex, single or in clumps, fading into far-off blue hills, with unknown desert behind them. One can hear the odds being shouted: "Seven to one *Mullalyup*, *Manjimup*, *Boyup*! *Chorkerup*, Charlie" (this last to the bookmaker's clerk). "Man Jim" is a name that has all the symbolic overtones of Ned Kelly, and if there aren't legends about his prowess as a jockey, even though handicapped by weight (for Man Jim, surely, was no stripling), it's time there were.

After the races, particularly those near the towns with their womenfolk and settled family life, there would be some kind of enormous feast, a *Wellbungin*, perhaps, or a *Bungulluping*. Indeed, even in the Australia of those days there may have been some fragmentary beginning of the urban ennui and discontent that runs through America today, when instead of an infinite, vague land to the west, a fluid and adventurous frontier region, all they have is Los Angeles, as municipal as Nuneaton; and tough, bearded bushwackers, regarding such a bourgeois function with incredulous scorn written all over their leathery features, would refer to it as a *Yabberup*, fit only for a lot of *Nambling* milksops and Poms.

Many such, like the roving heroes of *The Summer of the Seventeenth Doll*, would put off settling down to such faintly shameful domesticity (in a *Dwellingup*) until well into middle age. For them, even at such outlandish stations as *Wungong*, where the single general store, run by a Chinaman, was the only place for off-duty relaxation, the great weekend function would be the *Noggerup*—or, not infrequently, the more boisterous and violent *Gingin*. One may easily imagine the rivalry caused in the tension of enforced male continence by the appearance of a rare single woman—such a one as the famous *Wilga Turnoff*, with her smouldering Slavonic eyes, brought to these outposts by who knows what nineteenth-century tale of oppression and escape and wandering. Her arrival would be quite enough to turn a *Gingin* into a *Punchmirup*...

Ah, legendary days! I daresay it's not at all like that now. All the same, I'm pretty sure that a place like *Damboring* is not in the least what such a name would imply in England.

1851

THE MAN WHO OUGHT NOT TO EMIGRATE

THE man who cannot shave without hot water, or pull off his boots without a bootjack; the man who cannot get up without a glass of pale ale in the morning, or go to bed without a "bashawed lobster", or devilled bones; the man who has never carried anything heavier than his cane or cut anything stronger than his beard; the man whose only sowing has been limited to his wild oats, and his only reaping to EISENBERG cutting twice a year his corns; the man who has never handed any other bill but a tailor's, and only knows what a spade is by seeing it in a pack of cards; the man whose only knowledge of "hedging" has been derived from the race-course, and of "harrowing" from a Victorian melodrama; the man who only cares for a horse as something to bet upon, and looks upon sheep as "creatures from the country" that are fleeced at *écarté*; the man who imagines a bull walks on two legs like those he has seen on the Stock Exchange, and whose skill in shooting has been restricted to a few shots at the moon; the man who merely knows a bank and a rake from what he has seen at a *rouge-et-noir* table; the man whose footing in society has always been upon the very best polished leather boots, and whose longest walk in life has been through the Insolvent Debtor's Court; the man who has never known what it is to earn a dinner, or to enjoy one without French wines; the man who would think himself degraded if he was seen carrying a parcel:— such a man of all others ought not to emigrate. Better far for him to lounge and loll on sofas, and lisp, and smoke, and yawn in the country that can appreciate him, doing no harder work than digging occasionally in the morning papers, or on the gold districts of his mother's pocket, than to carry those same qualities to a distant land where they would only be thrown away, like early purl before quakers. Such a man, we repeat it, ought to be the very last in England to emigrate!

THE WILD COLONIAL BOY

Alexander Frater

THE other day, while buying roses, I met, through the auspices of a buddy who promptly faded, a prism-eyed, supple-thighed lass from the NW3 bloc. I swallowed my gum, mumbled Nicetameetcha and stood chomping on a split fingernail. Conversation proceeded haltingly till, with reference to a passing camel, I mentioned I was an Australian.

The dame teetered on a spiked heel and examined me with frank disbelief. "You?" she said.

"Uhuh." I straightened my shoulders and did a shambling little dance right there in the street. "I'm a cobber, I'm a mate, a Jimmy Woodser, a pannikin boss."

"You gonna sweep me off my feet?" she said.

"Well," I said, looking up at my reflection in the sky and trying desperately to get some semblance of toughness into my frozen, mawkish grin. "Some other time. Right now I must go home and gargle."

"You don't look like a Aussie," she said. "I mean, you're not tanned and all. You haven't got big, calloused hands or wrinkles round your eyes and your riding boots aren't scuffed?"

"They're not riding boots," I said with shy pride. "They're sneakers made from the underbelly of the warthog."

"You trap and skin it?" she asked. "The warthog?"

"No, I didn't. I hate the sight of blood."

"You mean to tell me you've never shot an abo?"

"I've never even seen an abo," I whispered. "Though I know the principle on which the boomerang operates."

"It comes back," she snapped.

"You know that?"

"Sure."

We stood tensely on the pavement while waves of busy burghers washed around us; she stared at me, her bright eyes clouded with suspicion; I wanted to take her hand and tell her she must not disturb the ordained order of things, that the world was dead on course, that she must not hurt herself, for had I not played chess on the very beach where Herb Elliot had romped as a stripling? But a tiny, sudden pulse in her throat warned me she was going to wound us both.

"Who's going to win the Test Series?" she asked. The voice was infinitely soft and sad.

I combed desperately through the bubbling morass of my mind, snapping at snippets which had accumulated like lees through the years. Dear God, I prayed, let me be right; if I call America let it not be the bloodsuckin' Russians or Serbo-Croats. I drew a cheroot from my money-belt and groped for my lighter. Drawing a deep breath I eyed her through the pumping thumb and shower of sparks.

"Armenia," I said.

Her mouth trembled. "You're a phony," she said, huskily. "You're compensating for the fact that you're stunted."

"No! I am what I say. Listen, I

once dropped a can of beans from Sydney Harbour Bridge and watched it burst; my grandfather saw Lassiter the prophet ride into the desert and I knew instinctively in the cradle that the platypus was a mammal. So help me, in Gundagai I saw one suckle a frog."

"You've been reading your *Guinness Book of Records*," she said. "Leave me now; go and gargle."

I turned brokenly and shuffled homewards, knowing I had failed her, knowing too that I was a raging disgrace to the sunburnt country. Right there in Finchley Road I prayed for a miracle of metamorphosis; I asked for many things, including the ability, rare in mongols, to conform to the beautiful image. When my heart had quietened I determined to tackle the transition logically, in phases. Speech. Work on the vowels, buddy, flatten them and shout to the winds a thousand times a day: *wash your fice in the bison* then listen critically to your echoes. Spirit of independence. Walk right up to a cop and tell him he looks shoddy and unshaven; I spotted one but he smiled and tipped his helmet as I approached so I beamed back and postponed the confrontation indefinitely. Muscular supremacy. I started to run, lifting my knees in the orthodox fashion, primarily to see what it felt like and for a while it felt OK, but ten strides made me weak and bored and I regretted the fetish and its place in my birthright. Sobbing to a halt I knew, absolutely, that I was stonkered.

It had been like this for some time. I am quiet by nature, perhaps even a shade imperceptible, and people are inclined to snort disbelievingly into their cups when they hear my country of origin. They will not accept my reticence for what it is (reticence) and, because I am shy, regard me as some kinda bastard. Staring at my weak eyes and small, crumpled body they want to be told that it happened at the age of three

"Tell me, man, how did the aborigines ever get into Australia?"

when I took on a battalion of Jap snipers with my bare hands. It's the same with my stutter; they stand there, the Pommies, aching to hear that I fell a furlong from home in the Melbourne Cup and got savaged by a thoroughbred but I've only seen the Cup on TV and then the reception was unusually bad. They will not accept that I am nervous about crossing streets and susceptible to attacks of acute depression, that I sleep poorly and with my window locked against burglars, that I undergo an emotional crisis every day when confronted on the Tube by a woman who wants my seat and I decide, agonisingly, not to give it to her. They will not accept that I am gentle, that I have a superb sense of protocol and exquisite manners, though I do occasionally chew crystal which pleases them.

What really hurts is their eagerness to give me the benefit of the doubt, to find excuses for me. When they fail I am resented because I am not loud and drunk and bronzed, a man who emerges from the cactus to fill his gut with beer, swap a few dry witticisms with the postmistress, who is as gnarled as a gumroot, then sprint the ten miles home in twenty minutes to sink a couple of artesian bores before tea and head off a thousand stampeding cattle. All this without feeling the need for a deodorant. I read books and love chamber music and there is something wrong.

When I got home my wife shouted: "Stop looking beaten!" so I did a ululating expression of the Wild Colonial Boy and, taking my cello bow, stood in the centre of the room and made like Bradman. I decided to get me a bush-wacker hat with a snap brim and a surfboard to carry through the city. But will it help? I am me, Samantha, not my country. And you, abandoned there on the milling pavement, must make allowances for the fact that environment doesn't work on everybody. If we ever meet again by the rose stall I shall take you by the hand and introduce you to a friend of mine, an Afghan who hates mountains. He thinks Armenia will win the Tests too, though he's not going to put any money on it.

THE KANGAROOS

THERE is a (Kanga) rumour
That sixteen Kangaroos
In first-rate fighting humour,
In cricket caps and shoes,
With bowlers out to fool us
And cunning bats and fields,
Are sworn to (Kanga) rule us
And see that England yields.

Our wiles will all be needed,
Our every (Kanga) ruse,
Before these guests are speeded
Upon their homeward cruise,
All day they'll feed the scorers
And keep their pens a-swing,
All day to cheer their fourers
The (Kanga) roofs shall ring.

Our nights we now must squander
From early eve till late
In sitting down to ponder
And (Kanga) ruminate;
But if we end by getting
A team to take us through
There'll be no need for fretting
And nought to (Kanga) rue.

April 21 1926

Up and Down Under Style

BARRY HUMPHRIES

THE only time I ever hear from *Punch* is when they want a pithy and confrontative essay from one of my celebrity stable; usually the actress and swami Dame Edna Everage, or the street-wise Chairman of the Australian Opera and Cheese Boards, elder statesman Sir Les Patterson.

But this time the editor insisted that a print-out from my own word processor was what he required, and I was so flattered I didn't look too closely at the subject.

Now I rather wish they had commissioned Dame Edna.

Style is a subject which actresses of all sexes can expatiate upon with the greatest facility.

In glossy periodicals between coloured photographs of wristwatches and beads, show-folk and shirtlifters (qv) are always keeping us up-to-date with what is or isn't camp, naff, chic, U, Sloane, un-cool, In, or vieux jeu.

Whenever an editor wants something on Art Deco cuff-links, drag, Haitian food, deleted show albums, Portugese baroque gardens, Susan Hayward movies, Zemlinsky string quartets, Diana Cooper, AIDS or Mother's Day, he touches a key on his computer and the names of a fastidious few shimmer chartreusely on his display screen.

And if a little epicene expertise with a Down Under flavour is required, my name, it seems, flashes. Australian Style is a daunting theme which few, admittedly, would dare to tackle.

Irish Cuisine, Swiss Humour, the English Work Ethic and the French Resistance—all seem like a push-over by comparison. For to most cultivated Europeans Australia is the Ultima Thule of philistia. Little wonder that over a million persons attempted to emigrate to my country last year; all fugitives from the Tyranny of Stylishness. All of them desperate to escape from a decadent world of after dinner mints, Princess Di look-alikes, gold credit cards, Quentin Crisp look-alikes, South Molton Street, Fifties furniture, re-appraisals of Arnold Bax and *The Thorn Birds*.

It is universally believed that Australia is a kind of health farm for the Art-sick. A drying-out clinic for the cultural lush. Aversion therapy for aesthetes.

No individual is more to blame than I for promulgating this scurrilous myth.

I confess that my original intention was merely to depict my countrymen as "rough diamonds" so that my own painfully rehearsed sophistications and puny sophistication and puny accomplishments might shine more brightly. For years I sold Australia short for my own financial gain, letting no opportunity pass when I could portray my people as oafish tosspots, sentimental, inarticulate bores, shrill, mindless, harridans and gross, slobbering, flatulent, flag-waving blatherskites.

My huge European following lapped it up. The fraudulent Australian stereotypes I presented on stage, film and television were just what the public wanted. There was a race of boors and buffoons Down Under that the Poms could safely patronise.

But today the game is up.

The Pershing missile has made a joke of distance, and distinguished British journalists and music hall artistes are now flocking to Oceania and discovering with surprise and not a little indignation that the image of Australia which I have for years promoted is nothing but a catchpenny fiction.

There is, in Sydney, a luxurious motor-inn much favoured by visiting celebrities—or, as we are called in Australia—Personalities.

On a typical day one might encounter in the lift Jean Rook, Gary Glitter, Jeremy Irons, Mary Whitehouse, some Pythons, Cilla Black, Algy Cluff, Red Adair, Billie Jean King, Alan Coren, David Bowie and entourage, Elton John and entourage, Lord Lucan and Charles Aznavour (sans entourage).

Between the eighteenth and nineteenth floors, whilst patiently waiting for oxy-acetylene torches to liberate them from their overloaded vehicle, the survivors may invariably be heard trading superlatives on Sydney's world-class personalised T-shirt shops, and its globally-known, hand-crafted. authentic kangaroo-fur souvenir ice buckets.

For whenever Top People meet these days, Australian Style is the talking point.

Clothes, generously cut and of world-class craftsmanship, are amongst the first things noticed by the envious visitor to Australia. Most ambitious young men work for some ramification of the Public Service or Film Industry where neat, clean, casual clothes are *de rigueuer*. Gone is the apocryphal, half-naked, lager-swilling lout of yesteryear. In his place—if indeed he ever existed—stands the typical new breed of Australian executive: sport-loving, culturally aware, articulate on the excellences of his superlative home-grown table wines, but above all, fashion-conscious to the point of foppishness with his modified Paul McCartney-style haircut, Dennis Lillee-cum-Zapata moustache and macho lobe-stud (weekends only).

When an Australian businessman expansively orders a whole bolt of powder-blue gaberdine-style fabric from his preferred Singapore tailor, he invariably creates the same sensation in the shop as do Australians in English butchers when they purchase an entire leg of lamb; but although a lucky few still shop overseas Sydney is Australia's style centre. It is the city which pioneered the lilac-ruffled dress shirt months before that item of apparel found favour with the Greek-Cypriot bridegrooms of Adelaide.

The womenfolk, too, have long ago cast off the boots and haversack of the European hitch-hiker and they are now the independent yet supportive wives and de factos of Sydney orthodontists and Trade Union executives. Apparelled by world-class Melbourne courturiers and on nodding terms with the *libretti* of the standard operatic repertoire, young Australian womanhood is a far cry from the valium-addicted one-sex-orientated kitchen drudge of yesterday.

A pioneer in the cultural revolution which has overtaken my homeland is the Prime Minister, Robert Hawke, who has—to use an aphorism popular with the media—put the S back into Australian Style.

A man forged by the working class, as etymologists and grammarians will at once perceive, Mr Hawke is, contrary to a misprint in the *Guinness Book of Records*, a teetotaller. However, on Dyonysian occasions of national triumph such as the America's Cup Victory (qv) he permits his drip-dry suit to be saturated with another man's spumante. In the sporting panorama he is as familar as the grandstand, and in his few months of office he has given his country such a deep sense of security that the once popular colour khaki has vanished from the fashion spectrum.

Our charismatic (qv) new leader is living proof that Style and Good Taste are not necessarily synonymous. A further instance of this was recently vouchsafed me at a formal dinner party in Canberra where a distinguished High Court judge expressed poignant concern for his wife's fluctuating health. "I'm worried about Maureen," he sighed, "just lately she's been up and down like a toilet seat."

Not, perhaps, a remark in impeccable taste, but surely an example of vintage Australian Style.

"Then there are our cultural bonds with Australia, our reliance on its football to keep our pools alive during the summer . . ."

Dateline Sydney

Soon after the Russians annexed Afghanistan, Punch *sent* ***ROBERT MORLEY*** *there to cover the Third World War. This was his first report.*
He seemed to have stopped over in Australia, God knows why.

THE first thing that strikes a correspondent in Sydney is that there are very few Russian troops to be seen on the streets, at least during daylight hours. What fighting has taken place has been extremely sporadic and despite the claims of the military that the occupation is now complete and the position once more stabilised, the population around the Kings Cross section, normally a vast tourist trap alive with sex shops, adult movies and girls in the traditional costume of shorts and see-through T-shirts, is still plainly ready for anything.

There are persistent rumours that the Prime Minister was executed in Melbourne in the early hours of last Thursday and that his subsequent appearance here on a local chat show to emphasise the necessity of abandoning the Olympic Games was a brilliant feat of impersonation by our own Ronald Barker who is, or rather was, currently resting in the city from his exertions after a successful appearance at a local theatre and is now being held incommunicado along with Messrs Corbett and La Rue and Richard Emery.

Australia has always been the second, third and often retirement home for English comics who traditionally succumb, after a long and successful career, in local motel bedrooms dead to the world. There has, of course, never been much communication or love lost between the various far-flung state capitals of this vast continent, so it is difficult to substantiate reports that Adelaide surrendered without a shot being fired, and that Brisbane is still fiercely resisting a strong Russian Armada originally disguised as a visiting swimming team.

Sydney, of course, has its celebrated harbour and the people here traditionally take to their boats at the first sign of trouble. As I look out over the majestic panorama towards the Opera House, still happily intact, sailing boats and sail-boards and motor launches crowd the water and if one didn't know what was happening, one might mistake the activity for some enormous regatta. The yachtsmen themselves occasionally come ashore to take on fresh supplies of beer and to light defiant bonfires on which to grill the local fish and sausages, keeping a wary eye open for any patrolling Russian gunboats in the vicinity; perhaps most extraordinary of all is that cricket is still being played on almost every available patch of ground not already in use as a bowling green.

There is plenty of time apparently to finish the game and fight the Russians as well.

There is a fellow who stays in this hotel, or at least commutes from it, called Brearley, a small, bearded poet bearing an almost uncanny resemblance to Ronald Duncan and whom I run into occasionally in the bar dressed in a kaftan. What W. G. Grace would have made of him I cannot imagine. He seems to be, or believes himself to be, Captain of England and is constantly shepherding his playmates, with the exception of one called Boycott, into a bus en route for yet another uneasy confrontation with West or possibly East Indian fast bowlers. He is keeping a low profile on the ground, while the aptly named Boycott is constantly declining to board the buses or show up anywhere except for book-signing sessions. The bookshops also appear to be still open. Apart from the failure of communication already noted, there is no doubt that the occupying authorities are imposing a rigorous censorship as if determined to keep the ordinary citizen unaware of what is happening.

The newspapers, far from carrying blank spaces as is more usually the case on these occasions, fill them with fantastic accounts of imaginary happenings; thus the front page of the leading Sunday newspaper displays a large photograph of a cricketer clutching a seagull. Bird and ball, travelling for once in opposite directions, had previously collided and play was halted, one read incredulously, until the seagull felt sufficiently recovered to fly off. Perspicacious readers will no doubt delight in this barbed allegory. This nation may have been temporarily stunned into aquiescence, but who doubts she will fly again one day?

Not all the messages are so clear, and I confess I was initially puzzled by a story on the back page of the same paper which I quote verbatim: "A Sydney girl who recently started work with a Hong Kong firm (in Hong Kong) reports by letter that she has to take her own loo paper to the office." Although lavatory paper in this hotel is still in good supply, I am now busy stockpiling.

In an even more subtle attempt to alert the reader, it is announced that a Mr Roger Climpson has undergone an operation to have the bags removed from under his eyes, Mr Climpson is, of course, a newsreader and explains in an interview that it was a long and complicated operation involving the removal of some of the skin from above the eyelid and tightening the skin below.

"It is quite common in the industry," he added, "and now I no longer look as if I had a row with my wife." His wife, who was apparently unavailable for comment, may, one suspects, be working for the enemy. Meanwhile the warning is clear. Do not believe all you see on television, where hopes for the new season are pinned on *Jonah*, described as "a series about a hunchback bootmaker living in Redfern" and *Rottnest Winter* about "a new family of Australian Shellducks hatched during the winter storms on Rottnest Island".

What has all this to do with the war, you may ask, and if I have to concede not a great deal, my readers must share my chagrin at being the only *Punch* War Correspondent in recent years who at the time of writing is unable to find the war. Only yesterday, taking a leaf out of the book of more experienced colleagues (for up to now I myself have been more a critic of food than carnage) I hailed a taxi and commanded the driver to go in search of guerrillas.

We drove through the shuttered streets (but not too much attention should be paid to this for the shops normally close here on public holidays and this was one apparently) and came eventually to a sort of car park where, to my surprise, an admittance charge was demanded. Someone has to pay for the war, I remarked cheerfully, as with some difficulty I manoeuvred myself through the turnstile. I was somewhat shocked to find that others who had come to see a part of the action were actually accompanied by children. Ah well, years ago children were taken to public hangings and I don't suppose what they were going to see would be much different from the sort of violence they watch nightly on television, but all the same I don't think I would have been able to forgive my parents if, at a similar age, they had conducted me on such a saguinary expedition and I had inadvertently stopped a bullet. But then, of course, I wouldn't have had to.

Well, to cut a long story short and slightly reduce the cable charges, I soon realised that the terrain the loyalists had decided to defend was some sort of zoo, but as usual they had apparently gone under cover and I was obliged to enquire of a youth wheeling a barrow of what looked like horse manure, but might just possibly have been some other compound with more deadly intent; bombs are made of the most unlikely substance these days.

"There's only one f...ing guerrilla as far as I know," he told me, "over there," and pointed to a small building in the distance. Discouraged but determined, I made my way in the direction he indicated. All these people and only one sharpshooter; but then Australians are notoriously easily satisfied when it comes to spectacle.

I recalled an occasion in this very city some years ago when several thousands had sat spellbound one long hot afternoon watching a man, two dogs and four sheep manoeuvring among hurdles and no one except myself demanded the money back.

I pushed open the door of what, at first sight, appeared to be a monkey-house and there he was. Dressed in faded green denims and a regulation peak cap, he stood aloof from the crowds which surged around him, leaning incongruously on a broom handle and regarding a large ape which seemed almost equally to excite the attention of the public. It was some time before I could make my way through the scrum to tap him lightly on the shoulder.

"I am from *Punch*," I told him.

"Never heard of it, mate," he replied, "but we get all sorts here. Where would it be exactly?"

"Tudor Street," I told him, "just turn down Bouverie and you can't miss us. As a survivor of the Battle of Britain myself I would like to bring you, on behalf of our readers, a warm note of encouragement and support. Would you, I wonder, care to give me your name along with an exclusive interview?"

"Are you some sort of Newsie?" he demanded. This is a land of abbreviations. Musco for musicians, Garbo for dustmen, so why not Newsie indeed?

"I don't talk to Newsies," he went on. Anxious to reassure, I produced my Diner's Card. It was of no avail. "If you want to know the truth," he went on, "I'm moonlighting."

"Just as I hoped," I told him. "Could you tell me something of your experiences after dark?"

"Another bloody pommie poofter," was his surprising rejoinder, as he turned on his broom and made off through a small door marked Staff Only.

As always, I shall just have to persevere.

"Can't get near the bloody doctor these days."

OEDIPUS BRUCE

In Australia recently, a recommendation was made that incest between a mother and son should no longer be illegal. **ALAN COREN** couldn't help wondering what effect this might have on Australian literature.

ACT ONE

Enter Chorus. They are citizens of Adelaide. They have corks dangling from their hats. They are all dead drunk.

Chorus: Our mouths are like the inside of an abbo's trousers. We have all been walking through yesterday's lunch. We are as much use as an earwig's tit. What happened to last Wednesday?
Enter Barry, King of Adelaide, on all fours.
Chorus: Hallo, Bazza, you look like two ton of old fish-heads.
Barry: I've just been out in the fly box, saying goodbye to breakfast.
Chorus: It's not like old Bazza to honk the bacon down the pipes after a night on the frosty tubes. Old Bazza had a gut like a ship's boiler. We have seen old Bazza sink ten gallons of Mrs Foster's Finest without threatening the drainage. Old Bazza must be upset about something.
Barry: Too right! I was reading my horoscope in *Beer Weekly*, and it says where it's bad dos on the family scene this year, my flaming son is gonna flaming kill me, also beer could go up by as much as ten flaming cents a tube!
Chorus: Stone the crows, Bazza! Ten cents a *tube*? This could spell the end of flaming civilisation as we flaming know it!
Barry: Next thing you know, the supermarkets'll be charging corkage on flaming Parozone! I blame the Japs.
Chorus: Too right. What's this about your son? We didn't know you had a son. We didn't realise you ever went near your old lady. Isn't she the sheila who looks like a '37 Holden pick-up, sounds like a drag-saw, and smells like a dead dingo?
Barry: Time was. She's past her best now. Still, when a bloke's tied a few on a Saturday night, it's no worse than cleaning the chimney in your bare feet. That's how we ended up with young Bruce. He's a bright little bastard, can't be more'n ten months old, and he's already been done twice for being in charge of a push-chair while unfit. I'll be sorry to see him go, straight up.
Chorus: Go? What are you gonna do with him, Bazza?
Barry: I'm not risking some flaming kid growing up and doing his

daddy with a lead sock. I'm gonna drive him out to Broken Hill and nail him to the floor.
Chorus: Good on yer, Bazza! Trouble with kids today, they need a firm hand. No flaming authority left. No sense of family. Good luck, Bazza, got to rush now or they'll be picking bits of bladder off the ceiling.
Exeunt.

ACT TWO

The outback, near Broken Hill. Enter King Barry, carrying Bruce, and Wayne, a shepherd. They are all drunk.

Barry: There you go, Wayne, I've tied his flaming feet together, all you have to do is drop him in the sheep dip. Watch how you handle him, he can go off like a flaming mortar when he's had a few, we had to redecorate the entire bungalow once.
Wayne: Count on me, Bazza. I'll pop him in the dippo when I go to fill up me bottles. I'm expecting a few blokes over this evening for a bit of a blast.
Exit Bazza. Wayne stands holding the baby for a moment or two, then falls down and begins snoring.
Bruce: Burp.
Exit Bruce, crawling.

ACT THREE

Twenty years later. During this period, Bruce has been brought up as a sheep by an elderly ram and ewe who found him as a baby. He walks on two legs, but neither he nor his adoptive parents think this in any way odd. This is Australia. Bruce's diet has been grass and sheep dip. He is tall, strong, and permanently drunk, and has picked up a little English from the labels of the beer cans with which the outback is strewn.

It is a hot morning. Bruce is staggering along a dusty track, when he meets another man staggering towards him. The man is Craig, a brewing representative. He is drunk.

Craig: Stone the flaming crows, it's Bruce!
Bruce: You got the wrong bloke, blue. My name's Sixteen Fluid Ounces. It was Pull Ring Here for a time, I'll give yer that, but it's never been flaming Bruce.
Craig: Well take it from me, cobber, it's Bruce now all right, they had your picture in *The Daily Beer*, and if you want my advice you'll keep away from your folks. It says in the paper that as sure as flies lay eggs in a wombat's trade-mark, you're gonna fill in your old man and marry your old lady!
Bruce: Yeah, well, the bloke who wrote that never saw my old lady. She's got four black hooves and twelve nipples, not to mention some

bloody peculiar personal habits. You'd think twice before jumping on a mattress with that.
Craig: Don't argue, mate, *The Daily Beer* never lies!
He falls down. Bruce hesitates for a time, then shrugs, sets his shoulders, turns his back resolutely on Broken Hill and takes instead the opposite direction, towards Adelaide.

ACT FOUR

The road near Adelaide. A battered truck is rattling along it, with King Barry at the wheel, lurching in every pot-hole and spilling beer-cans at every yard. At the top of a little rise stands Bruce albeit unsteadily. As the truck approaches, he thumbs it down. Barry looks out of the window.

Bruce: Afternoon, sport. You wouldn't have a tube of Foster's aboard by any chance? I haven't eaten for six weeks.
Barry: Well, now, blue, that's a very interesting question! A very interesting question indeed. Why not have it engraved on brass and shove it where the moon never shines, har, har, har!
At this, Bruce tears the door off, drags Barry out onto the road, and batters him lifeless with it. He removes eight cans of lager from the body, drains them, belches happily, climbs into the truck, and sets off on a zig-zag course, back towards Adelaide.

ACT FIVE: Scene One

A month later. Adelaide, before the royal palace. It is an attractive wooden bungalow with a pleasing neo-Georgian room-extension in primrose mock-stucco nailed to the front. There are five carriage lamps on the front door, and a gnome holding a sign that reads "38 to 38A Alopecia Avenue". Enter Bruce, who pushes open the wrought-iron gate and rings a doorbell. The chimes of Viva Espana die away, the door opens.

Bruce: Queen Glenda?
Glenda: That's right. Sorry about the Marigold gloves, sport, I was just worming the cat. What can I do for you?
Bruce: Promise you won't laugh, Glenda, only I met this sphinx up the road.
Glenda: I know how it gets sometimes, blue. I usually gets pink spiders running over the flaming sideboard.
Bruce: No, straight up, Glenda, I met this sphinx and it said if I got three riddles right I could come round here and marry you. I didn't have anything else on this morning, so I thought, what the hell, it's better than a poke in the eye with a sharp stick!
Enter Chorus, supporting one another.
Chorus: He'll be flaming sorry he said that!
Exeunt, on hands and knees.
Glenda: So you answered the riddle all right, then?

Bruce: I don't know. The sphinx was legless. It was all he could do to give me your address before he fell over.
Glenda: I swear they put something in it up the factory. When I was a girl, you could drink thirty-one pints before breakfast.
They marry. The wedding reception goes on for nine weeks. At the end of it, the bungalow has disappeared beneath a pyramid of beer cans. A number of guests are dead.

Scene Two

Some of the cans clatter to the ground. Bruce emerges from the gap, obviously distressed. He has a stick up his nose. Enter Norman, a neighbour. He is drunk.

Norman: Stone the flaming crows, Bruce, what's that stick doing up your conk?
Bruce: I've been trying to poke me flaming eyes out, Norm. I can't seem to get the flaming range. I guess I'll have to wait till I'm flaming sober.
Norman: You don't want to go poking yer eyes out, mate. They'll rob you blind up the off-licence. It could cost a flaming bomb! What made you think of it?
Bruce: I found out Glenda's me mum, Norm. I've only gone and married me flaming mummy!
Norman: No cause to pop yer headlights, blue! Mind, I can see it could be a bit awkward. Been a few naughties, have there?
Bruce: Nothing like that, Norm. Nothing of that order. I haven't been capable, for one thing. Glenda says they put something in up the factory. No, it's giving up the bungalow, Norm. You spend twenty years as a flaming sheep, suddenly you got gas central heating and three flaming low-flush pastel suites, it's not easy to give it all up just like that.
Norman: Strikes me you're being a bit previous, cobber, I can't see why you and Glenda can't make a go of it. She's a very nice woman when she's drunk and no beard to speak of.
Bruce: But it's against the flaming law, Norm!
Norman: Then they'll have to flaming change it, mate!
Bruce: Would they do that, Norm?
Norman: Would they . . . ? You just come down the pub with me, cobber, we'll wake up the Home Secretary and put it to him straight!
Exeunt. Enter Chorus, dragging one another.
Chorus: In Australia, all is flaming possible! In Australia, a new world is flaming born! In Australia, I flaming will! In Australia . . .
They collapse. They lie there. They snore.

CURTAIN

Turning Up Down Under

GEORGE MELLY

WE arrived in Perth at 2.00 a.m. Nevertheless we were met by the director of the Festival, David Blenkinsop, an example of courtesy beyond the call of duty. David is a Yorkshireman, a perfectionist, has little time for prima donnas, and a fierce passion to make each festival as lively, diverse and interesting as he can. There is a boyish side to him too, not immediately apparent behind his neat features and executive glasses. We were to become true friends.

We woke next morning to a blue sky and a gentle breeze off the Swan River. At breakfast I was spotted by a short, stout, elderly man who approached me with that direct friendliness which is perhaps the most universal Australian characteristic. "Ain't you the jazz feller that's headin' up north?" I admitted it was so.

Immediately after Perth we were to play four one-night stands on the edge of the tropics. "Seen you advertised on television," he explained. "Come from Paraburdoo meself. Nice place. Nice people. But hot! You'll need an icepack to sit your arse on. I'm down here on leave. I've got a beaut hangover. Daren't trust meself shaving. Glad to have met you."

His handshake and the size of his breakfast said much for his powers of regeneration. His name was Danny Beck and on his belt buckle was the representation of a massive truck-lift.

At 1.00 p.m. there was a press conference for John Chilton and me in a rather grander hotel than we were staying in. We were taken there by one of David's sidekicks, a girl called Sherry. Warm and open, practical, sensitive to our need for reassurance, we were all to fall a little in love with her. We expressed this according to our natures: John with old-world courtesy; Chuck with ebullient spontaneity; Barry by letting out information not absolutely essential; "the young 'un", Bruce Boardman, by following her around like an orphaned lamb; me by much hugging.

The press conference went well, and some radio interviews later that day managed, in David Blenkinsop's phrase "to put bums on seats". In between radio interviews, I walked the streets in successful pursuit of braces, for mine had broken and it seems that they are a means of keeping up trousers unknown to the belted masses of the Far East whence we came.

Perth is on the surface a rather staid old lady. It was only on our return to play a week at the Festival Club that I was to discover she could let her hair down and kick up her heels. There are high-rise buildings, mostly in the business section, but also much Victorian architecture, both monumental and domestic, pierced by shopping arcades. Green parks run alongside much of the blue and seemly River Swan, while beyond the Chirico-like railway stations is the great modern art gallery guarded by its obligatory Henry Moore, and most of the better restaurants.

The only blow we had received so far was that our gig in Melbourne had been cancelled. This was especially disappointing for Chuck Smith as he has a brother there he hadn't seen for seventeen years. That evening, while we were waiting for the others to stroll over to the concert hall, Chuck suddenly sprung into the air with a wild reiterated cry of "shit", and rushed across the lobby to embrace a new arrival with rib-crushing intensity. It was his brother Brian, who together with his wife, Sue, had unexpectedly flown in from Melbourne—well over a thousand miles—and I imagine, seeing the expression on Chuck's face, he must have felt that it was both money and time well-spent. He has done well in Australia, and owns a beautiful house outside Melbourne, where he breeds racehorses. I did wish, however, as I broke my nails on Australian airplanes trying to get little wedges of sweating Cheddar out of their clinging transparent envelopes, that he had made his fortune at something other than plastic packaging.

Our first Antipodean concert took place in the Perth Concert Hall, a large modern building of glass and brick, the hall itself enclosed by wide corridors broadening out here and there into bars and seating areas. At first the audience seemed rather bemused by my loud check suit, linking announcements and indeed choice of material, but gradually loosened up and we got our encores. After the hysteria of Hong Kong I was uncertain as to how well we'd done but the next day everyone said how much they'd enjoyed it, and the review in *The Western Australian* was a rave. It was, however, on our return a fortnight later that we really took off.

We had two free days before the mining towns. We saw Cleo give an immaculate concert, floating on stage in a Beardsley dress. We were invited on yet another boat trip with fellow artistes including "The Black Theatre of Prague", most of whom turned out, rather disconcertingly, to be called George. John appeared on a forum on Jazz in Britain, and the next morning at 6.15 a.m. we boarded a comparatively small plane and headed north.

Port Hedland, Paraburdoo, Karratha and Newman are all several hundred miles apart, the first and last on the coast, the others inland. They are owned by mining companies who hack out vast quantities of rock rich in iron ore and export it to be refined in Japan. The companies are like feudal barons, but very benevolent ones. They realise that to keep workers happy in that climate there must be plenty of diversion, good housing, air-conditioning and excellent wages.

We hadn't much idea of what to expect. In the event the towns resemble suburbs without a city: neat bungalows with green lawns, leisure centres, rather basic motels with swimming baths, local radio and TV, supermarkets, good roads. The mining operations lie a mile or two outside the dormitory areas.

The heat is appalling. Getting out of the plane at Port Hedland was like walking straight into the steam room at a Turkish bath. We wondered why, as we walked across the tarmac, the bronzed giants in shorts seemed to be sending out some mysterious form of semaphore. We soon found out. It was to drive off the persistent swarms of small flies, a gesture known as the "Australian salute". A French woman told us that when she first arrived she thought how friendly everybody was. She had imagined they were waving.

Self-contained suburbs and outside them the bush, a vast prehistoric landscape, cracked, raw, and breathtakingly beautiful: pink earth, olive grey trees, fold and fold of flat-topped mountains, and gallars, grey parrots with pink breasts, hurling themselves through the air in raucous dementia.

At each town we were received with great friendliness and much hospitality. My version of myself as Oscar Wilde lecturing on Rossetti, lily in hand, to the miners of Leadsville, needed adjustment. The audiences were quick and very receptive. There are lots of Poms working up there including many Liverpudlians. A big bouncing girl called Yvonne showed up that first night in Port Hedland. Did I know Adrian Henri? She'd been on an avant-garde film course with him. The leaving of Liverpool with a vengeance.

We flew to Paraburdoo in the small hours, the sky lit up by great flashes of sheet lightning. While were were asleep in the motel there was a tropical rainstorm. It didn't make it much cooler but it wiped out the roads. As a result the truck with our sound equipment and Chuck's drums was unable to get through, but an SOS on local radio solved that one, and Richard Meggett, an amiable, bearded sound engineer who was travelling with us, performed miracles. Not that the evening in Paraburdoo was without its trauma. The air-conditioning in the hall had broken down and they opened the sliding glass doors along one wall. Brightly lit as we were, the effect was predictable. The stage became an entomologist's dream. Silver stick insects, eight inches long, things like biplanes, praying mantises, and smaller but lethal bugs homed in on us. Apparently a visiting soprano, faced with a similar situation a month before, had fled on a high C. Later, I was to erupt into bumps.

The other concerts, while less hazardous and in larger halls, were much the same and the applause heartening. The people in these towns live a curious life. Some come, as they believe, for a short time to make their pile but stay for years unwilling or unable to break away. They drive you out to show you, with a certain pride, the chewed-up landscape of the vast mining operations, but in this enormous wilderness they look marginal. They join committees, play every sport, organise theatricals, live well, but they see you off at the tiny airports with a certain wistfulness. Here and there you see a group of Aboriginals, the dispossessed Red Indians of Australia.

I shall never forget those four days: the cheerful and plump Pom lady who told me her speciality was imitating Sophie Tucker; the touchy Australian police sergeant slumped asleep at a party with a "stubby" (small squat bottle of beer) clasped firmly in his outstretched hand; the big schoolmaster with his admirable unsentimental ethics; the ex-Liverpudlian local radio employee with so much sensitivity under his sharply cynical surface; the Wild West ambiance of the huge saloon-bar in Karratha, known locally as the "animal room", on a Friday night, (passing through in my stage suit to retrieve my hat from the restaurant, I was greeted by a barrage of kissing noises, whoops and guffaws).

We flew along the coast to Perth where we were to spend the night en route to Sydney. Beneath us the land looked like a full-scale map of itself. The sea was a cerulean blue broken by irregular patches of pale fluorescent green over the reefs. Perth seemed cosy and reassuring. It was almost like coming home.

Larry emigrates to AUSTRALIA

AS SEEN ON BBC 2

INDOCTRINATION CLASS
BEER

ENGLISH
IMMIGRANT
BITTEN BY
MAD DINGO

WAGGA WAGGA

SHEILAS
→

QUEENSLAND
SLOW LEFT ARM BOWLERS REQUIRED
N.S.W
CONSULT THE FLYING DOCTOR IF YOU HAVE ANY OF THE FOLLOWING
CHELTENHAM SPA 11,200 MILES

THE NEW AUSTRALIAN ANTHEM

In 1972, as part of his election campaign, Gough Whitlam promised Australian voters an alternative to 'God Save The Queen', to be chosen by competition. Miles Kington submitted this entry on behalf of *Punch*.

Australia! Land of boundless opportunity!
We praise thy rolling surf and shining sand.
Australia! Home of gum and eucalyptus tree,
Where bluntness goes with toughness hand in hand.
Raise high the foaming can of ice-cold Aussie beer!
Throw it at the umpire if he's wrong!
We want no bloody pompous Englishmen out here—
There'll be no jokes about convicts in this song!

What though the foreign monarch holds her sway o'er us
And makes us print her portrait on our stamps,
—No Aussie now will ever sing her graciousness,
And if he does, we'll sabotage the amps.

Let all sing out the joys of being Australian
And each man praise his country as he ought!
If pommie bastards try to call us alien,

They'll only make a ghost town of Earls Court.
So raise your voice—half Cockney, half American—
And let each cobber utter joyful sounds
Till e'en the bush repeats this haunting Strine again:
One New Guinea's worth a hundred old-style pounds!

What though the foreign monarch etc.

And see the *Sun* rise up above yon northern sky,
Its daily circulation in our sight now caught,
And hearken to the prophet, Rupert Murdoch, cry:
"Just give the Pommies murder, sex and sport!"
They're welcome to it—we'd rather with our sheila be
And crack a can of frosted Foster's beer,
Or grab a gun and persecute the wallaby
Or harbour lustful thoughts of Germaine Greer.

What though the foreign etc.

Australia! Graveyard of the British comic act!
The tomb of Hancock, Milligan on tour!
We've no desire to see your funny men, in fact
—You gave us Cook, so please don't send us Moore.
We may act tough and yet we shock so easily
(The Aussie's manly cheek soon blushes red);
At least we think our full and just revenge to be
That you got Barry Humphries back instead.

What though etc.

So hump your bluey, celebrate the billabong,
And hymn the Aussie despite all his faults.
Although you can't interpret half this silly song
And couldn't ask Matilda for a waltz
And know, like most Australians, that you've never seen
A kookaburra laughing up a tree
—For God's sake never tell a true blue Englishman
Australia's not the place it's said to be.

What etc.

Note: Foster's is not beer but lager. Lager, however, does not rhyme with Germaine Greer.

Australia and How to Cure it

QUENTIN CRISP

THE jokes that Londoners make about Wigan, in Sydney are flung at Brisbane; but it was there that enlightenment seemed to have dawned. I am standing innocently in my hotel room looking down at the doll's house churches nestling among the skyscrapers that are a feature of this city. The telephone bell rings. My caller explains that he is attending a school in which his class has been told to write an essay about a television documentary programme showing my arrival in Australia. This piece of information is in itself astounding. In England no teacher would set his pupils such a task unless he were more interested in publicity than in a steady job.

With what argument could he convince a board of governors that a subject so scandalous was merely a test of syntax and punctuation? Yet, if education has any purpose other than to become the most expensive time-filler in the world, it must be this—to induce uninformed minds to control their prejudices by means of words. When the term "sophisticated" is used of machinery in outer space it seems to mean elaborate; applied to a person, it means simple in the best sense of the adjective—direct. An educated man is someone who has survived his emotions.

More amazing, however, than the shadowy figure of this hypothetically enlightened teacher is the very real student. Apparently without any specific prompting from his elders, he is prepared to nag his sister into driving him a half hour's journey into town so that he may embellish his thesis with details gathered at first-hand from me. He has mentioned the name of the school at which he is studying but, as I have been in Queensland only a day, the information tells me nothing. I am therefore unprepared for the advent of anybody quite so young—fourteen at the oldest.

I realise instantly that, having still nine weeks to do in Australia, I must not figure in a sixth form essay beginning, "When I met Mr Crisp in his hotel bedroom ..." To avoid this, I ask my visitor to accompany me to the theatre at which, in an hour's time, I am to perform. I think that my dressing room will provide a marginally less questionable venue. As I go on to the stage in the clothes in which I walk through the streets, there will be no ooh-la-la behind an inadequate screen. Backstage I answer all the young man's questions without, I hope, saying anything which, if repeated by him, will cause either his father or his headmaster any alarm.

Nevertheless, our conversation is by no means humdrum. "My friends say that you're a slob," my interrogator remarks without hostility. He has noticed that my shirt is held together with a safety pin. I agree and the interview passes pleasantly.

Had he known it, it was a good night; there are times when I seem to be wearing chain armour.

In Melbourne I stood in the entrance to a cinema waiting for a taxi. Near at hand, two young men discussed whether they had or had not seen me on television a few days earlier. When they decided that they had, one of them approached me and shook my hand. After an exchange of pleasantries, he says, "So you're homosexual. Big deal." If these words were intended to mock anybody, they were aimed not at me but at the world. The phrase expressed the same liberality—the same blandness as that evinced by the previous adolescent—but in shorthand.

I am aware that Australians are famous for having invented the boomerang and for climbing impossible mountains but, even so, the intrepidity of these two young men amazed me. There were both at an age when elsewhere things are at their sniggering worst. On the platforms of Clapham Junction station, schoolboys squeak my name and, when I slowly turn toward them, they scamper into the nearest waiting room.

Everywhere you go in Australia, once it is known that you come from England, you are asked what you think of the place and its inhabitants. The question is put in a slightly hesitant voice as though expecting a rebuff. On one occasion, I was openly invited to consider the whole continent a cultural desert. I am the wrong kind of person to bombard with this kind of interrogation; to me culture is any television programme too boring to be advertised as entertainment. I am more interested in sophistication. If this is the quality that Australians feel they lack, they need have no fear. They have only to wait for the young men mentioned above to grow up.

What makes this national self-doubt the more disturbing is that it is felt in a land where happiness (for which culture is a poor substitute) grows on trees. The streets are paved with opals and, even in Newcastle, laughingly called "soot city" by my guide, the air is bright as diamonds. There and everywhere else in this earthly paradise, it is never colder than an English spring; the houses are clean as they were painted; the vegetation, as green as in an everlasting May and in places covered with camellias as big as cabbages. In the cities, the thoroughfares are wide and lined with trees as graceful as birches. Furthermore, in keeping with this setting, everyone is rich; the trains are empty but the aeroplanes are full—chiefly of men carrying in plastic covers their board-meeting suits.

Why then have the denizens of this Elysium become a nation of Madame Butterflies, forever standing by the shore with their eyes focused on the far horizon? Why is it that, when you arrive at any airport, it is as though you had come to save the entire continent (even at seven in the morning)?

I pointed out to a reporter the fact that Sydney is no further from New York than New York from Sydney. Reluctantly she agreed. Then since no one, I said, in New York sits sighing that he is so far from Australia, why do you perpetually complain of your remoteness from America. I suggested that distance was in the heart. The lady wrote down what I said but she did not seem convinced.

When trouble comes, England will lie flat on its belly in the dust of humiliation trying to avoid being caught in cross-fire exchanged by two giants both of whom it has made the mistake of trying to placate. Then, at last, Australia will realise that being thirteen thousand miles from the madding crowd was a hidden asset.

Of course, it is not impossible that all this self-deprecation is just another example of sophistication manifested by my schoolboys. It may be a polite ruse intended to prevent foreigners from feeling that they have lost face in the presence of such coast to coast prosperity.

If, on the contrary, this continental malaise is real, I have a simple remedy to offer. It is purely a convention that north is at the top of all our maps. Why do we not, for the next hundred years at least, agree to print our atlases the other way up? Then Australia would no longer occupy the invidious place of an anthropological footnote. Instead, it would be the opening paragraph to the history of the world.

"Best pickpocket in Kalgoorlie!"

We Hunt the Kangaroo

A.P. HERBERT

December 9 1925

WHEN I say hunt I do not mean hunt, and when I say kangaroo I am told that I should mean wallaby or wallaroo. With these exceptions however the above title stands.

Whenever we see an Australian newspaper-man he says, "What are your impressions of Australia?" and I reply, "It is too large;" and George adds tactfully, "And much too far away." Since we landed on these genial shores we have travelled three or four thousand miles, yet when we peep at the map of the place our track looks like the track of a snail which has dithered for a few minutes on the outside edge of the Oval. We have simply hovered on the fringe of a small corner in the south-east. It is true, as I said to George, that this is the corner in which the men of Australia live ("And the women, old boy," said George), and we like them too much to be exactly crazy about the places in which they do not live. However, after a long course of inspection sugar-factories, butter-refineries, saw-mills and saw-mines (by me), and an awful lot of dancing and horse-racing (by George), we decided we must have at least a glimpse of the vast open spaces, the immense natural resources, the back-blocks and the places where life is life. But however far we go we are invariably told that this and that is very fine, but of course we have not seen the *real* Australia. And it is my suspicion that there *is* no real Australia.

To reach the "sheep-station" we had quite a short journey. Just 8 a.m. to 10 p.m. in the train and a hundred-and-twenty-five miles in a motor-car—nothing more. Why, in this country there are people who travel two hundred miles for a tennis-party, knowing, the fortunate creatures, that it will not be raining when they arrive. The Queensland Railway has a gauge of three feet six; the trains upon it make much more noise than the Tube; they rock like babies, but roar like lions, and the passengers converse by signs. Also it was perfectly evident to me during every minute from 8 a.m. to 10 p.m. that the next moment the train would leave the lines. George disagreed; he said that for about a fourth of the day he felt perfectly safe. The New South Wales Railway, on to which we changed after dinner, has a wider gauge, and the passenger, if still alive, can frequently hear himself shout. Let me add, however, that the trains themselves are exceedingly comfortable and well served. One only wishes one was deaf, and wonders why one isn't.

Motoring in the vast open spaces is even more exciting. One passes rapidly from bump to bump, rising violently in the saddle. The reason why Australians are so expert at broncho-busting is not that they do

so much riding on horses but that they are constantly riding in motor-cars. For there is nothing between the motion of a bucking horse and the motion of a good car on an average country road. The only difference is that the horse tires at last, while the car goes on for ever. To be any use in this country a car must be capable of anything, a fact which, it is hoped out here, our British manufacturers are now assimilating. It must be able to fight its way through morasses and travel cheefully in a cloud of dust and creep for miles in a couple of ruts, and open gates and kill snakes and frighten cattle off the roads and climb cliffs and, if possible, trees. And it would be just as well if it could say a prayer or two. For it is a rule of the road in Australia that the rougher the surface the faster the driver goes. There is so much land about that for long stretches there are two or even three alternative tracks, made during the rainy season (if any); and I have noticed that at these places our genial hosts invariably select the track which reminds one most of the Arras Road, no doubt because it generally gives them an opportunity to charge down a bank and travel for a little while on two wheels.

When they come to what is called *good* road, they just crouch down over the wheel (if there are no cattle or sheep or wild horses in the way) and let her rip, turning finally with a gay glance at the speedometer to remark, "Touched sixty then". And I always wonder, if that particular sensation was produced by touching sixty, what exactly would have happened if we had hit sixty properly. "Speeding" in Australia is not a vice, it is a religion; and some of the young ladies and all the young men are among the most devout. "It is said," said George to one of his drivers after about ten breathless miles in which we had touched sixty, a hen and a couple of stone bridges, "that you have so few English cars; but it is perhaps fortunate that you have no roads." The driver never spoke to him again.

George is incorrigible. After a hundred miles our host turned off the main road through a gate to call on a friend. After about a hundred yards he found that he was not on a side road, as he supposed, but in the bush. An Englishman might have paused, or even retreated; but on went the Australian, undaunted, murmuring casually that he had "missed the track but thought this led in the right direction." So on we went through the bush, cannoning from gum-tree to gum-tree, plunging into pits and crawling up the other side, climbing over fallen logs and ant-hills and rolling always like a ship upon the tempestuous Tasmanian Sea. What happens in these circumstances when a car breaks down I do not know, but it seems that no car does break down in Australia. However, when even this indomitable machine paused for a moment before an insurmountable bank and it seemed that it might be our fate to be bushed in a motor-car and our bones picked by the jolly green parrots that flew about us, not to mention the eagles that hovered further up, our driver turned his head and said mildly that he was sorry for our sakes that he had left the road. George opened his eyes and, looking about him, said sleepily, "I didn't realise you had." One of these days George will almost certainly be deported.

It has taken so long to reach the sheep-station that now I cannot tell you about the kangaroo hunt. Reach it we did. But the sad thing was that after all these miles and adventures they told us that we had not yet arrived at the *real* Australia. this lonely and cosy old house in the bush, they said, though it might be a hundred miles from a railway station, was further still from the genuine "back-blocks" which are another few hundred miles to the West, and as for the "out-back", that, it seemed, was another good hard fortnight's motoring. It is as I suspected. The real Australia is always somewhere else.

Meanwhile the lonely old house in the bush was inhabited by charming hosts of good British stock, with English books and English newspapers, and even the domestics were new-come from Scotland.

"George," I said as we gazed in the failing light across the vast open spaces, "shall we go on to the out-back? Shall we take car again and ferret out the back-blocks? This is not the real Australia, George. This is practically England."

"And quite good enough for me," said George.

So we stayed. But we were not so easily to escape from motor-cars. In the dusk five kangaroos of monstrous size came out of the scrub and grazed upon a "rocky knob" above the house. And our hosts took us out to get a closer view. And I saw ourselves creeping thrillingly up the hill on our stomachs to approach the engaging but nervous marsupials, Indian-fashion, up-wind (or possibly down-wind?) But not a bit of it.

"Get out the car!" cried Bill excitedly.

"The car?" I echoed stupidly.

"They will let you come much closer in a car than if you are on foot," was the astonishing reply.

"Goodness!" I cried, "is even the kangaroo——?"

But they drove the car up the rocky knob. And it was so. And as (from the car) we saw for the first time a wild "old man," a great dark beast, erect, and kingly and apparently unafraid not fifty yards away, a certain note of sadness was mingled with the thrill.

"*Et tu, Brute,*" I whispered mournfully.

"Is it a *real* kangaroo?" said George innocently.

Captain Cook Re-discovers Australia

An extract from the 1975 journal of the explorer's visit to the crisis-torn continent, presented by arrangement with E.S.Turner.

H.M. Barque Resolution

October 2

Rounding Cape Dissipation at dawn we dropped anchor again off that Doubtful Land now called New South Wales, the discovery of which, as many assert, has lamentably failed to enrich the human race. In Sydney Harbour the needle of the compass seemed to be afflicted with dementia, as if all the laws of Nature were thrown into confusion. The cause lay in the existence on the harbour floor of immense deposits of beer cans, jettisoned by the besotted heathen from their sail boats.

Great God, this is an awful place! On a spit of the harbour the natives have assembled a vast idolatrous monument, compounded of concrete sails, which they proclaim to be an Opera House. In the catalogue of human folly it eclipses the statue of Ozymandias, King of Kings. More than three hundred lotteries were held to raise tribute for this extravagance, a fitting memorial to the spirit of gambling which animates an unregenerate land. The building, if rumour speaks truly, is to be used not for opera but for a decadent sport entitled Rollerball.

Rising above Sydney is a giant stalk with a drum balanced on top. The drum is a fashionable chop-house which rotates through 360 degrees, thus enabling the diners to miss no feature of the scabrous landscape. It is a conception of fathomless imbecility well calculated to appeal to a primitive people anxious to impress its neighbours. Baubles like this do little credit to civilised realms, but here, in a land which can think of no better names for its townships than Woolloomoolo and Koolyanobbing, God is truly mocked.

October 4

The natives still retain an artless simplicity, but it is difficult for the philosophical mind to hold converse with them. Their articulation is primitive and the rhythms of their speech are destitute of that pleasing melody that commands itself to a cultured ear. They address all persons of whatever rank as "cobber" or "sport". From the frequency with which they invoke the Supreme being I am persuaded that they are not ungrateful for the sparse bounties of Nature, but if they entertain any fear of future punishment it is not apparent in their demeanour. Boastfulness is the principal defect that sullies their character. The men, to judge from their vociferations when drunk, appear to hold chastity in little estimation.

Last evening the crew returned with evidence that horrid rites are still practised, in particular the custom among adult males of knocking out each other's foreteeth. A lusty, tattooed rascal who ran amok uttering wild blasphemies threw himself into the harbour, whence he was rescued by two of the gentlemen from Resolution, *whose foreteeth were knocked out for their trouble.*

October 5

Today a burly son of Nature called Go-ugh, who is distinguished by the title of Prime Minister, visited Resolution. *He is not wholly lacking in those rational qualities which ornament the human mind. To these he adds a ferocious cunning and high scorn for his enemies, who are seeking to deprive him of revenues with which to conduct his administration. Go-ugh has never heard of the Paw of Subordination which alone renders*

human intercourse agreeable. Tainted by liberal notions in his youth, he still hopes to establish an egalitarian society in these Antipodean realms. He resents strongly any suggestion that his land is ungovernable and even asserts, with unbecoming effrontery, that the Land of the Great Queen is in no better condition. As he left the vessel, he compounded his impudence by suggesting that we might be better employed in seeking the North-West Passage.

Several of Go-ough's council of chiefs in Can-ber-ra are thought to practice a form of concubinage, but this is not yet widespread among the common people, among whom the rumours are likely to create an unwholesome spirit of emulation.

October 8

On enquiring what had happened to the Aboriginal inhabitants of Australia, I was informed that they had been hunted down and their tails turned into soup. This is typical of the difficulty encountered by the stranger in his pursuit of exact knowledge in these savage climes.

October 9

This day I ventured into Sydney in a horseless vehicle. As I sat down in the rear seat, the driver, a clownish fellow, turned round to enquire whether I was of the opinion that his breath smelled or that his socks needed changing, or that I supposed him to be a poofter. Eventually I discovered that it is the custom to sit alongside the driver as a demonstration of universal brotherhood. On subsequently enquiring whether a poofter was an evil spirit I received replies which were ribald when they were not evasive. Whatever it is, the men profess to hold it in abhorrence. They are ever on the alert to detect the presence of poofters, notably in the guise of Poms, as they are pleased to describe Englishmen.

On my visit to Sydney I was allowed to enter a temple to the goddess Chance, where hundreds of men and women were trying to extract pitifully small coins from garish machines by pulling levers. A not uncomely young woman who I judged to be a housewife had blisters on her palms as if she had lately been rowing a long boat in heavy seas. It is an affliction known as jackpot itch, for which there is no cure but abstinence.

October 11

Aboard Resolution *this day came a chief calling himself Dr Jim, who boasted of his plans to make his continent the colliery of the world. However, before he can mine the coal he requires a loan of uncounted millions from the Sheikhs of Arabia. How true it is that the climate of this unhappy land scorches and destroys the minds of those who dwell in it! Dr Jim is as mad as a bandicoot. He admits that he has forfeited the favour of Go-ugh, but he still entertains hopes of bringing unlimited riches to his land at a stroke. The gentlemen of* Resolution *humoured him as far as they were able, and, as he left, the midshipmen counted the spoons.*

October 13

Dropped anchor at Bondi Beach, which is inhabited by a swaggering race of sun-worshippers. Neither males nor females take conspicuous pains to conceal their pudenda. *The crew of* Resolution *were in a state of great excitment at sight of the well-formed Shee-las, as the women are called, and had to be battened below for the good of their Christian souls. Many of the older Shee-las, though lacking in that delicacy which distinguishes the European female, nevertheless affect some degree of modesty.*

For our entertainment, there was a parade of Life Guards, young men of heroic mould whose function is to save all but poofters from the jaws of sharks.

October 14

A message received this day from Go-ugh. He sends me tickets which entitles me to travel in a "train" called the Indian Pacific to Perth, journeying for more than two days across treeless desert. When I enquired, "What is at Perth?" they said, "We were afraid you would ask that. It is the City of Flies." Declining the tickets, I asked what other amusements they could provide for me. They said there was an exceptional platypussary at Melbourne, a town which also has relics of the great legislator, John Stonehouse. As an alternative, they pressed me to follow in the footsteps of Ned Kelly and Ben Hall, two desperadoes who have become folk heroes. The banks and post offices raided by these men have been rebuilt so that their deeds may be commemorated to eternity. What a truly perverse people! They have even reproduced the likeness of the convict-architect Francis Greenway on their currency.

October 16

Rumours of coups and revolutions in Canberra. I judged it expedient to raise anchor and set sail for home. The crew fought off a number of voluble young men who wished to be shipped as supercargoes to Britain, where they hoped to become entertainers, or to set themselves up as critics of Western culture. From the quayside they howled at us in fury, denouncing us as a lot of bustards. The bustard is a bird indigenous to this continent and not yet exterminated.

November 10

Dropped anchor off Perth, City of Flies. Why do not the natives exterminate their insects, instead of their bustards and kangaroos?

There came aboard a rogue who wished to sell me a number of opal and zircon workings, together with a cluster of gold mines. He said that the ghost towns attached to the mines could readily be made populous again. I have clapped him in irons and shall release him on a lonely island, where he can no longer prey on honest mariners. Some day it may please the Admiralty to chastise this sinful continent, which has so weakened the faith of His servants in the perfectibility of man.

1853

Aristocracy and Its Antipodes

IF the Legislative Council of New South Wales are enabled to effect their proposal for the creation of an hereditary Peerage in that colony, it will be necessary to assign amorial bearings to the new noblemen. This will be no very difficult matter; respect being had to the origin of the chief families that will be comprised in that aristocracy. For example, here is the blazon of a coat that might be borne by the name of SIKES, elevated to the Dukedom of Norfolk Island.

Gules, on a cross *ermine*, between four handcuffs, *or*, a jemmy of the field. Crest, out of a window shutter *vert* a hand, *sable*, grasping a centre-bit *proper*.

The above coat will readily be seen to indicate that the founder of the bearer's family had been transported for burglary accompanied by violence. The latter feature of his achievements is denoted by the sanguinary colour of the field, and of the implement depicted on the centre of the scutcheon. By the number of handcuffs are signified two convictions. The cross alludes to crossing the herring-pond, and the ermine indicates the judicial sentence by which the voyage was prescribed. The crest speaks for itself; the use of the term sable is an allowable liberty, as being necessary to represent the probable state of the member to which it is applied; considered in relation to soap and water. The family motto might be, *Mortuus vivo*, which would be a neat paraphrase of "Death Recorded".

The horse, the sheep, the pig, and other cattle—for stealing which the forefathers of the ennobled parties were relegated—would furnish abundance of animal forms for the purposes of heraldic symbolism. To these might be added the magpie, the stoat, the weasel, and other creatures that are the emblems of theft and larceny. Though, for the matter of that, the more ancient devices of eagles, dragons, griffins, lions, and the like beasts and birds of prey, would do quite sufficiently well to glorify exploits of plunder and rapine; nor could any motto for the member of a Botany Bay nobility be more suitable than some of those very professions of ancestral principle, which are the glory of certain high pedigrees among ourselves. "Thou shall want ere I want," for instance, would precisely suit the descendant of a footpad. A convict who had become a prosperous gentleman, after having completed his sentence of transportation for seven years, could not have left a happier legend to his posterity, than “I bide my time.” Moreover, when it is considered that the foundation of not a few among our own great houses was either fraud or force, it cannot be asserted that a Peerage of New South Wales would not rest to a considerable extent on a like basis with the British nobility. So that, when you come to think it, there may not be so very much difference, after all, between those who came in with the Conqueror, and those who went out in the convict ship.

"He's not the dedicated physician he used to be."

Back in the Decadent Dump or How to Desert a Cultural Renaissance

BARRY HUMPHRIES

"THERE'S a Cultural Renaissance going on in Australia at the present period of time, and *I'm* not ashamed to be a part of it!" That awe-inspiring statement was flung at me, more in sorrow than in anger, way back in 1965 by some Melbourne Michelangelo when I was about to return to London to resume my sporadic theatrical career. Faced with almost inevitable poverty and failure in a dreadful climate I must have seemed perverse, if not mad, just walking out like that on a perfectly good cultural renaissance.

I suppose Sydney Harbour *tastes* not unlike the Gulf of Tuscany and, on a dark night after a surfeit of Chateau Down-Under, the Sydney Harbour Bridge vaguely resembles the Ponte Vecchio. For that matter, Ayres Rock is merely a larger version of Mount Parnassus painted tangerine, and the Sydney Opera House (in 1965 at least) was roofless and rubble-strewn, *just* like the Parthenon!

Similarly my Australian acquaintances were possessed of a Da Vinci-like vigour and versatility. They worked in advertising agencies, wrought telly criticism, reviewed pop records, edited savagely satirical magazines, ghost-wrote the autobiographies of surf-riders, and sometimes even took photographs. Although they struck terror into the hearts of local Philistines and craven expatriates, they were so obviously overflowing with creativity one would be foolhardy to reject their invitation and drop out of the downunder renaissance. Nonetheless I did. It was hard to deny convincingly that my motives for returning to the Great Wen were to crawl up the backsides of the decadent Poms, rubbish my old mates, and sell Australia short up the length and breadth of Britain.

I had known Australian painters, actors and writers who, having failed to crack it in the Olde Country, had preferred to starve to death in their Holland Park bedsitters rather than go home and face the scorn and derision of the cultural elite in Melbourne and Sydney. Pining for local lager and lamingtons (an ethnic cake; sponge cubes doused in chocolate icing and desiccated coconut) they sat before their guttering paraffin heaters quaffing costly Redoxons and staring morosely at their damp-ravaged Qantas posters. To rationalise their ill-fortune they blamed the Brits.

"They're scared silly of us, Bazza," said a wild-eyed duffle-coated Australian film-maker to me once. He was shivering with apoplexy rather than the cold. "As soon as my sister sends me the fare I'm clearing out this decadent dump. The Poms can't stand our bloody *vitality* and sheer creative bloody *drive*!" he added, sliding languidly from bar stool to Watneyfied Axminster, his fingers barely enclosing the pound I had guiltily lent him.

But Aussies who have made the big time in England become objects of pity rather than contempt at home. Rolf Harris, Sidney Nolan, Rupert Murdoch, Scobie Breasley, Joan Sutherland, to name but a few traitors to the Southern Cross have not *really* succeeded, certainly not in an arena where success counts for anything. They've *sold out*! Capitulated to English decadence, the fast sterling quid, and in many instances which shall be nameless, compromised their pure heterosexual Australian bodies. If they really get to be world-famous they cease to be Australians at all. Expatriate is the dirtiest word in the Oz vocabulary. Next to, and often synonymous with, poofdah.

SCENE: The V.I.P. lounge of Sydney airport. Kangaroo fur carpet, sharkskin upholstery, Aboriginal motifs on the Japanese vinyl wallpaper, vases of flesh-pink gladdies and trays of piping hot savoury lamingtons and ice-cold sparkling Queensland sherry. An Australian actor returned from London faces the Media.

Channel 5: Great to have you back, Bazz! Now you're back to Aussie how much can we expect to see of you?

ACTOR (*suffering from five consecutive champagne breakfasts and acute jet-lag*):
I'll only be back for three months I'm afraid, Ian. Been offered a BBC series

Channel 5: Yeah. I suppose your old mates seem pretty unsophisticated after the types you're used to rubbing shoulders with over there!

(*Brief pause for drinks*)

Channel 8: Great to have you back, Bazz! Now you're back in the sticks, how much can your old mates expect to see of you? Just a flying visit to syphon off a few dollars then back to Britsville?

ACTOR (*haunted-looking, but quick as a flash*): Cripes no, Colin! I mean, there's a bit of talk about a TV series, but what the hell. It's great to be back. Well, blood's thicker than water, and all this lovely sunshine... The beaches... Planning to stay on in Sydney indefinitely as a matter of fact. There's a cultural Rennaissance going on in Australia at the present period of time, and I'm not ashmed to...

Channel 8 (*interrupting with a friendly grin*): That figures, Bazz, that figures. The word's around you're not doing any good over there!

You can't win in the super-egalitarian society, and it's OK to walk tall* in Australia so long as you're no taller than anyone else. And yet, having opted

*'Walk tall in Australia': an exhortation to stunted Englishmen circulated in the late 1960s by the Australian emigration authorities.

for life in the Decadent Dump, one occasionally experiences a wistful twinge of nostalgia for wholsesome, rennaissance-style living in the Promised Land, flowing with milk-shakes and tomato sauce.

One misses dinner in a smart Canberra restaurant with the head-waiter wearing a dinner jacket over his cardigan and an ice bucket beside the table filled with tinned lager. One misses Brisbane television with its all-night horror movies and all-day horror commercials.

One misses Yugoslav taxi drivers and bank managers in long white socks and bermuda shorts, and the priority coverage which British royalty still receives in Australian newspapers and magazines. Long after Australians have learned to shuffle patriotically to their feet after the first few inane lyrics of *Waltzing Matilda*, the *Australian Woman's Weekly* will still carry the world's most authoritative documentation of the Windsor family, its dress and doings.

Living in London one also misses a society which is predominantly Anglo-Saxon; one pines for all those faces, sun-bronzed albeit white. Of course, the pressure of dwelling in the surging centre of a fully fledged cultural rennaissance has taken its toll of the once healthy and robust Antipodean. Next to his Australian cousin the Englishman seems trimmer and more rested. A meatless diet, and the admirable London custom of commencing the weekend on Friday and starting the business week on Tuesday makes for a more relaxed and ulcer-free white-collar population. The sensible habit of working in the office from 10.30 a.m. till noon and then from 3.15 p.m. till 4.30 p.m. with a civilized break for lunch, or leaving the phone of the hook or never bothering to answer it, all these deeply-ingrained customs keep the British businessman clear of eye, fresh-complexioned and free of those neuroses which afflict the frenetic work-crazed Aussies.

Poms who migrate to Australia usually survive if they remember to swim between the flags, but if the sharks don't get them, the pace and the protein will. Ten swift Frosties and a stand-up underdone tournedos isn't the Englishman's idea of a healthy lunch-break, and he's usually just started to pick at his prawn and pineapple omelette when the lamington trolley swings into view.

Australians are either eating on foot, or transporting tucker to their luxury bungalows in the suburbs. A nice little Brit migrant I know got a job driving a Melbourne taxi. One evening last month he picked up the Archetypal Australian-in-a-hurry outside a pub laden with parcels. Falling into the back seat of the enormous Holden the fare said:

"Take us home for cripes sake, sport! Have you got room in your cab for twenty beers and three dozen oysters?"

"Bung 'em on the front seat if you like mate," said the obliging Brit.

His intoxicated passenger put his chin over the edge of the upholstery and copiously did so. It took two cops and a bucket of Dettol to clear the cab.

I suppose one man's taxi is another man's vomitorium, and even a Rennaissance society has odd moments of something like decadence. For those of us who can't make up our minds whether we prefer the English or the Australian variety there's always Marrakesh or Manila with extra lengthy siestas and faulty telephones to suit the Poms, and for the delectation of displaced Aussies, plenty of taxis with convenient Jumbo-sized bucket seats.

ET IN AUSTRALIA EGO

ALAN COREN

Dateline: Burrewarra

ONE hundred and ninety-six years ago, they stumbled ashore, salt-caked and weevil-bearded, wove up the beach on rubber legs, squinted at the vast nothingness with tiny sun-shrunk pupils, and asked themselves whether the rap for nicking a ha'penny loaf was not, perhaps, a trifle stiff.

But, because they were made of the sort of stuff that would, one day, be able to bowl forty consecutive overs of homicidal bouncers, flat out, and still have enough energy left to kick an opposing batsman as he hobbled in for tea, they rapidly pulled themselves together, struck up *Lillibullero* on a whittled flying-fishbone fortuitously snared in the Timor Sea, and marched off to build the Coolangatta Motel, where I spent last night.

They did not, one must assume, know that they were building a motel. They thought they were building the first convict settlement in New South Wales, not perhaps appreciating that Australia would be, by 1984, so short on historical artefact to give it tourist clout that it would be forced to capitalise on its duff provenance and turn a few corrugated iron sheds into not only a shrine but a leisure complex. Or, rather, simplex.

It is, of course, the best place to stay if you have been to visit that other great tourist cynosure, the Kiama Blowhole, which I understand is well worth the long overland trek just to watch the sea-spray shoot sixty metres into the air through a hole in a rock, which apparently it does quite often, except on those day's when you come fourteen thousand miles from Cricklewood to see it. On those days it is just a hole in a rock, even if you sit there for five hours waiting for the floodlights to come on, just in case it blows; but of course it doesn't, and what you are looking at is a floodlit hole, which, after another hour, begins to make you wonder what is on television in Cricklewood. The Kiama Blowhole was discovered by George Bass in 1797, on a day, obviously, when the spray was coming out of it, or he would never have discovered it and involved subsequent generations in vast expense on floodlights.

As there is not much else in Kiama apart from the Blowhole, by eight p.m. I was ready for the Coolangatta Historic Village Motel. Equipped as this was with all the domestic comforts of a pre-Victorian tin chokey, I did not go to bed immediately but shuffled instead to the dining-room, where they gave me a corner table next to a picture-window on the outside of which, in the top left-hand pane, a spider was spinning a web.

I say spider. It could well have been a crab in a ginger toupee. It was the size of my breadplate. As I ate, I could not take my eyes off it. Any minute, it could kick in the window and fight me for my steak. Not, indeed, that I ate a great deal, since the spider's own culinary arrangements tended to wither the taste-buds as they sprang: it does not whet the appetite to watch bugs the size of golfballs whanging into the glutinous hawsers from which a giant spider cobbles its dinette, there to await the mandibular crunch of an arachnid Stilson.

The waitress caught me gazing at it.

"Where does it sleep?" I said.

She did not, as one had rather anticipated, reply: "Anywhere it bloody likes", but merely gave that delightful Australian locution, "Beg yours?"

"What I mean is," I said, "do they get into the cabins?"

"We spray the rooms," she said, "but guests are advised to lift the lavvy seats as a precaution. Cheese?"

I shook my head. It was time to go to my room and get a good night's standing in the corner with a rolled-up copy of *The Australian*. I shall never again have a word said against Rupert Murdoch.

So, this morning, here I am at Burrewarra, jotting on the Holden bonnet. Since you will wish to visualise this, let me say that Burrewarra is a few miles south of Ulladulla and just before Murramarang. You may at this point be tempted to enquire why so much of Australia sounds like people being strangled, but you will not come up with an answer, unless it be that much of it was indeed founded by those given to strangling one another, so that the places were, quite simply, named after the first thing that came into their heads.

Or the last thing that came out of them.

Either that, or the smarter transportees whiled away the long voyage reading Swift. There could well be small towns all over Australia called Brobdingnag, Struldbrug, Houyhnhnm. Several called Yahoo.

What is totally beyond question is that this Pacific coastline is extraordinary beautiful: a thousand miles of wood-girt golden bays stretch south from Sydney, their only flaw being the fact that they are unspoiled. This being a travel number, you are entitled to expect the names of surfside hotels from which the lucky European who has fled the muck-infested shingle and the poisonous seas of his domestic costas may pad across the spotless sand and into the crystal water; but I have none, because they have built none. The little towns, like cloned Wembley miniatures, which string the coast from Sydney to Cape Howe, are all built just inland and are studiously non-resort. True, they have small dour commercial hotels, all built from flotsam in 1909, where travelling ironmongery salesmen drink tubes of Toohey's bitter and dream of the landlady's knickers, and they have more modern clapboard motels, air-conditioned, for snaplock junior executives in hired Hondas, *but they do not have one single seaside hotel!*

I had imagined, in this, our hugest colonial footmark, what? Vast Eastbournes, shimmering Frintons, limitless Hoves laid down by genteel expatriates nostalgic for mock-Regency facade and cherry whelk-stall alike—but there is, quite literally, nothing. A thousand miles of the finest beach I have ever seen, and never a shop to buy a Mickey Mouse bucket or a water-wing; a thousand miles of kiddy paradise that has never rung to the thwack of truncheon on Judy; a thousand miles of sea, without a pier.

I cannot unravel this conundrum. I shall make enquiries tonight, in Mollymook.

A bunch of the boys were whooping it up at the Mollymook Hotel, as Robert William Service might well have sung had he not, in 1894, turned left at Preston Slipper Baths and opted for Canada, but instead turned right and plumped for Oz.

Much of a muchness for the emigré back then, all in all: sharks or bears, bush or tundra, Ned Kelly or Dan McGrew. Flip the coin, Bob, flip the coin.

Had it fallen heads, he could well have been standing beside me now, clutching a dead gum tree for support and struggling to focus on the dawn-gilt ocean.

Last night was my second without sleep. Hardly had I stowed the mud-caked car beneath the welcoming lee of the Mollymook Motel and dragged my bones and bag upstairs, than I was pounced upon by a corridorful of cheery souls who slapped my back and who, as I unlocked my door and caught my first and last glimpse of the easeful cot, followed me in, bearing with them small plastic freezer-bags full of *tinnies*, this being the affectionate diminutive for ice-cold cans of aerated dingo-widdle which, ring-pulled, go off like premature grenades. Supped, they set the fillings dancing like Nipponese wind-chimes.

Enormously friendly, my new and unanticipated room-mates could not be refused (one is always, it must be remembered, terrified of confirming the image of the cheerless Pom); I drank their cryogenic mouthwash in vast quantity, and in the fullness of time, not to say bladder, we repaired to the Mollymook Golf Club for dinner.

What do those three capitalised words conjure up? A Mulliner night in a chuckling Sussex bar, swopped tales of the dog-leg fifth, elderly monocled lesbians plucking burrs from their Fair Isle socks, and Nicklaus-clad media executives telling lies about their XJ12 and their last mistress?

The sign in the little foyer of the Mollymook Golf Club read FORMAL CLOTHES REQUIRED FOR DINNER. MEN IN UNTAILORED SHORTS NOT ADMITTED. Upstairs, the enormous bar resembled nothing so much as the engine-room of a Cunarder running on beer: two-thirds of it was occupied by men in, presumably tailored, shorts, roaring at one another from brick-red faces, while the other third was a segregated enclave of women and girls shrieking and tearing at one-armed bandits with one hand and inflating their livers with the other.

"Bit flaming quiet tonight," yelled the motel ringleader in my ear, and then the peristaltic lurch of the mob hurled us against the bar, from which point on little that happened has remained in the memory, except for one of those ringing Australian circumlocutions that have done so much to advance the careers of chaps like Clive James who arrive at Heathrow with trunkfuls of such stuff and proceed to change the face of journalism as we know it.

Just before sunset, a man on whom I had been leaning suddenly grabbed my arm, and pointed beyond the bar window towards the sea, over which a huge khaki storm-cloud was swelling.

"You'll have to put a brick on your zip tonight!" he shrieked.

It took me some time, in my undermined state, to work out that what he was trying to tell me that the storm was likely to be so fierce as to cause serious damage to anything not securely tethered, among which threatened items the most precious was undeniably the contents of the tailored short.

In the event, when the storm broke, the raindrops came down like jellyfish. Our scurrying party arrived back at the Mollymook Motel soaked, at two in the morning. It wasn't until the half-dozen of us were back in my room that the ringleader suddenly smacked at his forehead and cried:

"Jesus! We forgot to have our flaming dinner!"

And opened another tinnie.

Do not think I forgot to ask them how it was that New South Wales had not built itself a Frinton or a Hove: it was simply that, somehow, the opportunity to raise the question never seemed to offer itself.

THE CONVICTS' REVENGE

The story begins 100 years ago when a gang of ex-convict guerillas led by Ned Kelly resolves to turn the tables on Britain, and robs banks to raise money for the cause. After the bushranger period C.A.I. fund-raising techniques become more sophisti Skilled agents infiltrate the home country's capital.

And their secrets are transmitted direct to the new C.A.I. headquarters—a vast underground complex in Earls Court, with secret entrance in an innocent all-nite laundromat. In the Fifties, the London intellectual world is duped by Sidney Nolan, who spreads the Ned Kelly myth under cover of an art exhibition. I Sixties, after a barrage of non-stop pop off the shores of B lasting several months, C.A.I. pirates swarm ashore and take Radios 1 and 2.

Mobs of Australian cartoonists undermine credibility of British politicians by vicious caricatures. Richard Neville's underground press cleverly avoids being illegal by being illegible. An alarmed government tries to stop the rot by rushing through immigration laws but the C.A.I.-riddled media forces them to recant. In a d coup top agent Edna Everidge, the Mata Hari of Moonee P introduces her accomplice "Goffo", a small-time movie actor, No 10, disguised as the incumbent Australian Prime Minis 'he incredible story of how the unknown C.A.I. (Convicts Against Imperialism) reversed the course f history is told by former agent ARTHUR HORNER

Thirties a notorious hit-man known as The Don is blazing ess trail of destruction through the country, from London ds to Manchester. The MCC is powerless. Later an invasion uthful racketeers engulfs Wimbledon—the courts soon resound to the activities of Kenny and Newc, Evonne and Rod. Joined by American mercenaries they force the LTA to disgorge thousands in "prize-money". Next, cadres of Australian dentists in Mayfair and Belgravia bug the teeth of unsuspecting V.I.P.s.

painter Rolf Harris raises a Youth Movement and makes a of didgeridoo attacks on the BBC TV centre, with heavy ties among viewers. Continuing the takeover of the media, R. Murdoch sweeps through Fleet Street making the popula press offers they can't refuse. With a beard grown for the purpose Clive ("Jesse") James does the same for the quality press.

est is history: primed with secret Cabinet information, a of grenade-throwing Australian commandos is able to ilate England on the field of Egbaston. England's leader is deposed, the whole population demoralised. The wheel turns ful circle: the first prisoners are soon on their way from Australia to the "mother country". The convicts' revenge is complete.

Dateline Melbourne

ROBERT MORLEY

DINING last night in Sydney with Mr Ellis Irving, an actor whom I have known for many years and whose word I can accept without question, I learnt to my amazement that the projected invasion (which I reported on a short while ago) apparently was cancelled at the last moment. No Russian troops landed in Sydney or anywhere else in Australia and whatever dispatches may have been received in Tudor Street, I am able categorically to deny. My "reliable source" and I had a most pleasant evening over mud crabs and a bottle of Riesling. The wine going down almost equally as well as the crabs, which by the end of the meal were deposited for a considerable distance around us. Bibs and finger bowls not withstanding. As is often the way with crustaceans, the meat is sweeter on the other side of the claw. The problem is how to crack the spidery shells and not grow too exhausted to continue feasting.

How pleasant afterwards to deal with a Pêche Melba and what a relief. There seemed little point in hanging on in Sydney, so have moved to Melbourne. The last few days in the New South Wales area have been extremely wet and windy. Hurricane weather, as the natives call it, but although the television has featured extensive floods and the inevitable movement of the elderly back to the schoolrooms and requisitioned drill halls, I really saw no point in adding, by close questioning, to the troubles of those whose homes had been carried away. The authorities here advise seeking refuge in emergency in the "smallest room of the house" but then which of us doesn't have to do so from time to time.

As earlier explorers have pointed out, Melbourne, the capital of Victoria (how these place names help in understanding the ambiance and period of all these cities), is situated on the banks of the Yarra River.

It is in fact no more than a leisurely flowing ditch and there is a popular theory that not only does it flow backwards but also upside-down; thus clear water is only to be found *under* the rather muddy surface. On its banks this morning I launched the annual "raft regatta appeal" in the company of two employees of a popular local soda pop factory dressed as Vikings and a raft made entirely of the empty tins in which the mixture is normally contained.

Several local television networks covered the ceremony and it must have seemed to them a welcome break from the happenings they normally record. For, in truth, this staid, rather placid backwater is also something of a permanent disaster area. In summer some part of the surrounding bush country is nearly always alight and the owners of charred properties are interviewed, against a background of acrid smoke by the side of gutted motorcars and burnt down bungalows, commenting on the fact that they just managed to save the mother-in-law but not alas the budgies.

In the spring they are baling out parlours or wading along newly opened canals, pushing improvised barges made out of packing-cases containing all their worldly goods with the possible exception of the piano, which floated off independently at the height of the holocaust.

In the autumn they are pictured standing on the roof which once sheltered their loved ones but now had been deposited by a hurricane a good deal further than they are able to carry it back.

What is so remarkable about the demeanour of those who will, hopefully, appear only once in their lives in front of the lenses of eager newshounds, is their quite extraordinary cheerfulness. Either all properties around here are grossly over-insured or the pioneer spirit still persists among the citizens and the knowledge that what didn't take much to knock down won't take all that long to knock up once more.

When disaster strikes the stiff upper lip is much in evidence. The fact that it is also firmly clamped to the lower one makes it sometimes difficult to understand what it was that actually hit them. Then, too, almost all Australian motorcars are natural killers; almost twice as many people die in road accidents in this country than anywhere else in the world—always allowing for statistical adjustment—but the motorcar out here has another even more lethal prerequisite, a long tradition of instant combustion. Parked amidst others on race tracks, beaches or picnic areas, they unaccountably burst into flames and thus start a chain of bonfires among other vehicles, causing the occupants, snoozing after a heavy meal or resting from the labours of love, to run for their lives. Australians are notoriously carefree when it comes to the disposal of litter or cigarette ends but it is generally accepted that motorcars often get so depressed at careless handling and too much exercise that, driven to desperation, they commit hari-kiri.

Melbourne is, of course, almost continuously strike-bound; one day it is the trams, the next the trains, on the third day both are struck, along with the fire brigades and the dustmen. Thus most Australians need their cars on weekdays to get to and from their work and to transport their garbage to a convenient tip, of which there is no shortage in these parts, but on weekends they simply get in them and go for a drive.

The sad thing is that with all the traffic on the roads and quite often in the nearby ditches, you never see an English model. Always a "do-it-yourself" nation, they like to be personally responsible for any breakdown which may occur. The Prime Minister, when he is not being unceremoniously butted by one of his own bulls, as was the case this week at the local cattle sales, is still actively campaigning to move the Olympics from Moscow to this city and one cannot help wishing he may succeed. Athletes have it far too good with all these carefully raked running tracks and deep sanded pits. It might do them good to hold their childish encounters in genuine bush country, vaulting kangaroo fences and pounding dried river beds throwing their hammers into impenetrable scrub land, running marathons in the local hills. This is presumably what the Greeks did when they first set out and the Australian Government would, as always, dearly like to put back the clock if unfortunately it hadn't already stopped, in the land where Lord Melbourne still rules.

I was all packed to visit Adelaide when chancing to turn on the television I was horrified to discover they were suffering from a plague of mice. Hundreds of thousands of the small creatures devouring everything in their path. I do not intend to come all the way out here to be snapped up along with the cheese and the grain, so thought it prudent to visit Canberra instead. Canberra is the headquarters of a peace-keeping force fulfilling much the same function as Brasilia. The politicians, diplomats and Civil Servants who serve their time in this extremely beautiful open prison are expected to impinge as little as possible on the lives of the ordinary citizens and although escape from Canberra itself is comparatively simple, most of the inmates resign themselves cheerfully to the enforced inactivity which the regime demands.

Built around an artificial lake and dominated by an enormous war memorial, the architecture varies from the grandiose early Lutyens to the late Nissen Hut. The latter built in the justified expectation of the growth of bureaucracy just after the war have, like our own prefabs, survived despite predictions that they would succumb in early childhood, and lived on to ripe old age.

The Houses of Parliament, like the present Prime Minister, are built of altogether sterner stuff. In the beautifully air-conditioned chamber, replete with mace and speaker in full-bottomed wig, Mr Fraser reclines in a swivel chair surveying his class like the headmaster of a good comprehensive school faced with the difficulties of a new term and some older boys who should have left long ago and continue to set a rather bad example to the newcomers.

Headmasters, alas, are seldom concerned with education. Administration is their game and Mr Fraser gives the impression that he personally could function a good deal more effectively if he was not for ever having to take time off to address the school. True, he delegates authority to his prefects, summoning them one at a time to sit beside him while he tells them what he expects them to say and how he wishes them to say it. They scurry off to the despatch box and clothed with a little brief authority, do their best to impersonate their master's manner and voice, the latter, alas, to these battered old English ears often proving largely inaudible. While I was there the Head spoke at more than his usual length about the way the Russians were generally letting down the side.

During this rather lengthy "pi" jaw the boys opposite were at pains to try and persuade him that his words were wasted on them, some of the bolder spirits repeatedly leaving for the cloakrooms without first raising their hands to obtain the required permission. Others slept while a number spent the time folding circulars and positioning them in envelopes, although no one actually interrupted the flow to request a stamp.

If Mr Fraser does not suffer boys gladly he seems more tolerant than most of his calling to parents and possibly elder sisters. His own wife and daughter and a row of beaming ministerial wives followed his every word with the keenest enjoyment and wrapt attention normally afforded to visiting dignitaries and The Master himself on school speech days. Unaccountably I dozed off, was tapped on the shoulder by a vigilant press secretary and conducted to the bar. We were invited for drinks later in the presidential suite but, alas, I had to decline as I had to return to Melbourne. I learnt, however, that Mr Fraser is surprisingly unpunctual; he catches aeroplanes at the last moment, confident that in any case they will wait for him and, like our own Mrs Thatcher, can be a trifle peremptory with those whom he feels are wasting his time of which, one gathers, there are a surprising number. Both, one feels, have the best interests of the school at heart.

To Australia for a Shilling *1852*

IN the race of competition for cheap fares, everything is outstripped by the announcement of a visit to the Australian Gold Diggings for one shilling. We have made the voyage, under the experienced conductorship of MR PROUT, and have enjoyed all the pleasures of the trip without the drawbacks of sea-sickness, short provisions, insufficient accommodation, or any other of the evils to which emigrants are liable. The passage is quite a pleasant after-dinner affair, and, instead of sitting over our wine at home, we have enjoyed the sample of Cape and Madeira drawn—not from the wood but from the water—by the clever artists who have united their talents in describing pictorially the passage to Australia. The intending emigrant to the Diggings will do well to go and look upon the true picture in Regent Street before he embarks for, perhaps a mere waste of time, on the waste of waters. He will then learn, not only the fact that all that glitters is not gold, but that gold itself may have the shine taken out of it by the hardships to be endured in finding it. Not that MR PROUT'S Diorama of the Gold Fields is likely to discourage emigration, but, on the contrary, to render it beneficial by setting people right as to what they may expect, and thus make it tolerably sure of their expectations being realised.

THE FIRST RAILWAY IN AUSTRALIA

1852

AN Australian paper gives an account of the start—and rather a "rum start" it was—of the first Railway in Australia. The line is called the Hobson's Bay Line; and from the account of the proceedings we should say, that in the case of Hobson's Bay, Hobson's choice has been realised. The Colony must be satisfied with the best it can get, though the Railway Line seems to be something quite out of the line of the Australians, if we may judge by the description contained in the following paragraph, extracted from the *Sydney Empire*, of the 18th of September:—

> "SIR CHARLES and LADY HOTHAM and a considerable number of the distinguished officials having taken their places in the train, which only consisted of four carriages, the signal was given to proceed. The steam was turned on, but the iron horse would not budge an inch. Great was the dismay depicted on the face of the engineer and engine-driver. The valve was opened to its widest extent, and the pantings of the over-laden steam horse were quite alarming. The band of the 40th struck up a merry tune to hide the confusion, but still the train would not move. Accordingly a whole host of railway porters and policemen set to work and pushed it along the line by main force for a hundred yards, when it again came to a dead stop. More police then came on, and a stout gentleman in a dress coat, ready for the banquet, came behind and applied his shoulder vigorously to the buffer of the last carriage, and at last, by slow degrees, the train moved, amid shouts of laughter from the assembled thousands in Flinders Street."

This is not exactly the way to go a-head in an infant Colony, and though the police may be considered to embody the great principle implied in the words "move on!" we do not think "the force" should be used in applying that principle to an obstinate railway train. Even the police, however, could not make the Hobson's Bay locomotive "move on!" and it was only when "a stout gentleman in a dress coat" applied his shoulder to the "buffer"—and it became a question of "buffer against buffer", that the train moved in earnest, and the old buffer triumphed over the new one. As it is probable that the stout party in the dress coat will not be always at hand to put his shoulder to the wheel of a refractory railway carriage, it is to be hoped that the Australians will get up their steam a little better than they did on the inauguration of their first Railway. Later advices are, however, not very encouraging, for a more recent extract informs us that:—

> "As the six o'clock train was leaving Sandridge a slight derangement occurred which prevented its progress, so that the passengers had to alight and walk up to town. The stoppage was understood to arise from some of the fire bars having fallen out, so that the fire could not be sustained."

What with an engine that won't strike out, and a fire that won't keep in, we fear that the railway system must be considered in a state of infancy, or even babyhood in Australia.

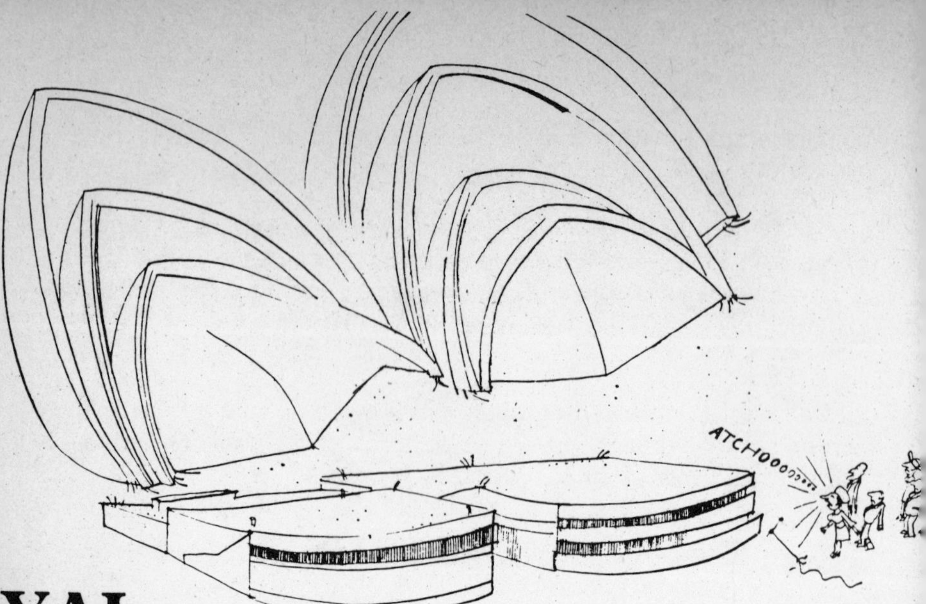

ROYAL BLUE

Having opened the Sydney Opera House, the Queen and Prince Philip staye[d] on for a short Australian visit. So did HEATH.

"Gentlemen, the Queen."

"I understand that without an assisted passage they couldn't afford to come."

"My cobber and I . . ."

"And this is the Earls Court Jester."

"He says if he doesn't get an invite to the wedding he's going to see that it rains."

"I hear they did arrive, but like true Poms got the next plane back."

The Earls Court Scribes

In 1975 the then Prime Minister Gough Whitlam introduced a scheme to subsidise Australian novelists. Alexander Frater charted the consequences.

ROSE at 5 ack emma, stewed a pan of tea bags and settled down at the trusty Olivetti with the Chandris Line Cabin Baggage sticker on its flank to conclude chapter three. Fine morning, tits warbling in their drinking coconut, Co-op Dairy bloke smashing bottles on the pavements as per usual, but feelings of pleasure and purpose marred by the silence. Once, at this hour of the day, you could hear the steady clack of typewriters sounding all the way down to Earls Court Road as a veritable army of pushy little sods got stuck into their Great Australian Novels, puffing away at Embassy Golds and absently picking their teeth with the coupons as they cast about for inspiration. These days, however, one catches only the odd desultory burst, echoing like sporadic gunfire, as the few writers—like me—unable to scrounge money out of Gough's new-fangled Literature Board, press on in the few free hours available to us.

The LB men, naturally, were still asleep. O'Toole, downstairs, is one of them. His monthly cheque from Canberra enables him to drink spirits, patronise the best massage parlours and add to his modest collection of French crystal. At nine he will rise and, after a leisurely breakfast, wander outside to polish his new MGB. Where is the justice in that?

Gough has a lot to answer for. Doubtless he dreams of presiding over a great cultural renaissance. He probably sees himself as a latter-day Medici, ushering in a brilliant new era of artistic achievement and humanitarian ideals. He wants to flush out the Tolstoys hanging around the Melbourne docks, the Beethovens and Da Vincis employed as airline clerks and supermarket cashiers, and allow the nation (and the Party) to bask in the light of their genius. But all Gough has done, in fact, is raise the rents in Earls Court. The landladies, who have good reason to bless him, employ the deluge of Aussie dollars to improving their properties. They are installing central heating, getting extensions built and fixing smart brass coach lamps by their front doors. The area shows signs of becoming exclusive, and the first question they always pose to new arrivals turning up on their doorsteps is, "Are you one of Mr Whitlam's novelists?"

And what is Canberra getting for its money? The other day, when O'Toole was attending a sale at Christie's, I sneaked a look at his MS. Rubbish? It was laughable. A dynastic novel, if you please, about a family of dentists who have practised, for generations, in a town up on the Murray. It opens in the 19th Cent. with the patriarchal figure of Doc Dunwoody (later to make a fortune from the Dunwoody patent saliva pump) treating the Burke and Wills Expedition for sore gums. He diagnoses scurvy and goes out for lemons, unaware that his wife, Ma Dunwoody, is at that very moment in bed with Rod Woollacott, the district's largest lemon grower. Woollacott, a handsome Old Etonian, has been banished to the Colonies for bringing a gorilla, inflamed with brandy, to an important social christening in Smith Square, where it had sexual congress with the font. Doc arrives for the fruit and walks into the bedroom with his empty baskets and there is a tremendous brawl and much bad blood which goes on for a hundred pages of the best linen-weave foolscap money can buy. It shook me up, it really did, and I passed the rest of the day in a state of deep depression.

But I digress.

My own labours progressed all right. I completed chapter three with my two main characters—picaresque, rather quixotic idealists who travel through contemporary Australia trying to put things to rights—sitting atop Ayres Rock, watching the sun set and wondering how to get down again. Then I ate my customary plate of Alpine and set off for the hospital where I work as a porter. It was an uneventful day, but for the fact that a man who looked like John Updike (for a brief moment my pulse raced) had a coronary thrombosis while I was taking down his particulars. I thought, from the noises he was making, that he had merely swallowed his tongue, and I called calmly for a spatula but, fortunately, a passing West Indian boilerman diagnosed the real trouble and the patient was saved. Such is the web and woof of life and, some day, I will doubtless put the incident to good use.

Back home I did an hour's revision, and cut the lengthy Socratic dialogue with the Lithuanian sailor washing his smalls in Rose Bay. Then I swallowed a tin of Main Course soup and took myself off to the Golden Nugget. They were all there. Gough's men, sipping vodka and flaunting their Gucci belts and Hardy Amies shirts, stood about in the Saloon Bar while the rest of us roughed it in the Public. Hennessy, nursing his half pint like a broken thumb, was looking doleful, as always. "How's it going, sport?" I asked.

"Terrible," he said, giving me a look of great cunning. Hennessy is mad, or pretends to be. Years ago Sir George Weidenfeld asked him the time in Trafalgar Square and Hennessy, whose watch had stopped, was unable to tell him. Now he is quite deranged, and has developed a nervous trick of winding his old Seiko every few minutes. This anxiety manifests itself in other ways, too. He is unable to get beyond page 2 of his book. Every morning he embarks on a completely new one, with a new plot, new characters, new locality, but then he abandons it and set off to earn his bread and scrape in the Harrods cheese department. But Hennessy is actually rich. *He sells his beginnings* and, since there are several thousand of them, there is no question but that his prospects are bright—particularly as they are snapped up eagerly by the new arrivals, flush with government money. Since Gough started his scheme Hennessy has never had it so good, and I sometimes wonder whether this mental blockage that afflicts him after 600 words is entirely voluntary. Now he caught my arm and whispered, "I've got a beauty here, son, right up your street. It has pace and attack. The prose is unusually spare, and the main characters are defined early on with a few deft strokes. Start your fourth chapter beautifully, it would."

"I can't afford your prices, Hennessy," I said.

"For you, son, 75p. Here, cast an eye over it. You'll see the possibilities, I'm sure."

So I did. Actually, it wasn't all that bad. It dealt with the rather disturbing notion that the youth of Australia are now eschewing careers in tennis and the Stock Exchange to become writers—and that they are coming here to do it. Hennessy had described a Qantas 747 touching down at Heathrow with several hundred of them aboard, all arriving to tackle the Great Australian Novel, and he posed the question: *why Earls Court?*

"I'll take it," I said.

I paid him and left, wondering too what awesome primeval instinct brought us clean across the world, like spawning salmon, to write our GANs in these shoddy few acres. And then, walking the desolate streets, it suddenly came to me. The secret lay not with Earls Court, but with Australia itself. Why did we feel such a powerful urge to leave? Gough would want to know that and, for a price, I would find out and tell him. I had nothing to lose. Everyone knows that fiction is dead. The future lies with the factual stuff, and a heavily-subsidised work of popular sociology, richly- illustrated, handsomely-bound and selling at about twenty dollars a throw, would make an absolute killing. But there would be important letters to write first and, turning for home, I began composing them in my mind.

Down Under and Out

FRANK KEATING

FORTHCOMING Australian cricket will be distinctly odd. No Test cricket side will ever again be Chappelled, Lilleed, and Marshed.

They left, as they arrived, together. They first played against Illingworth's England side of 1970–71. Thirteen years: an awful lot of Pommie-bashing. They didn't care at all for Pakistanis; they pitied little Indians and provincial New Zealanders; they snarled back, glare for glare, at West Indians; they might as well have got on famously with South Africans had they been allowed to play them. But it was Englishmen they loathed.

Forgetting, for a moment, that the word "cricket" still has, to some, connotations of chivalry, the three of them were quite superlative cricketers. Chappell, ever with an upright, cultured, haughty detachment, scored more Test Match runs than any other Australian—more than Bradman, more than Harvey or Ponsford or Trumper or Woodfull or Walters. Lillee, with the Kestrel's cruel eye, the ominous drum-roll run-up and the classic side-on action, took more Test wickets by far than any of history's legendary bowlers—more, by a bulging sackful, than Gibbs or Sobers or Hall, or Trueman or Tate or Underwood. Marsh, squat as a mudlark scrum-half, with miner's forearms and gymnast's sprung heels, dismissed many more Test batsmen than even such revered and glittering glovemen as Knott or Evans, Murray or Struddy, Grout or Tallon or Taylor.

They worked together. When Lillee bowled, the other two took the tandem in turns. The legend "c Marsh b Lillee" was inked into schoolboys' scorecards almost a hundred times in Test Matches—a staggering figure when you realise that history's next double act of bowler and padded henchman at the time was that of Botham and Taylor with 52—followed, by the way, by such appealing duos as Grout/Davidson (44), and Oldfield/Grimmett (37), one more than Murray/Roberts for the West Indies, and Marsh's separate swagbag with Max Walker.

And if Marsh didn't pouch the nick from Lillee, more often than not Chappell, at slip, would. In his last Test Match, Chappell beat Colin Cowdrey's record of 120 catches. Half of them were sponsored by Lillee's outswinger.

I saw them first on the Friday of the Lord's Test in 1972. It was "Massie's Match", when Lillee's Perth clubmate bewildered the English with his massive, gently curling, frisbee swingers in the heavy, clouded, atmosphere. At the other end, the gangling Lillee had looked angry and menacing and fast. That afternoon, England hit back: Australia lost their openers for seven runs: Greg Chappell, as palely frail and straight-backed as a model girl, joined his shoulder-rolling, gum-chewing, combative captain and brother, Ian. They shored up the innings in a stand of 70-odd, the elder man lecturing the kid between every over. Epic stuff. When Ian went, cursing, the young man—who had not scored a boundary in those first three hours—plonked his left foot down the pitch and dismissed Snow, Price, Greig, Gifford and Illingworth to all points. He went to his century in the last over of the day—and next morning he was joined by the tubby Marsh, who peppered the pickets with six 4s and two 6s in a merry half hour. They had announced themselves to England.

It was later on that tour that, by chance, I shared a lift with the young Chappell. We sat together in the back of the chauffeured limousine. I started with time-of-day small-talk, I received not a single word in reply. When we arrived at his London hotel, the Waldorf, he was asleep. I gently woke him. He got out, and slammed the door without a word to me or the driver. Ever since, I have been in awe, or certainly wary, of his cold-fish disdain.

Opponents, too, have been intimidated by his almost sneering silences. Tony Lewis said that he'd occasionally punctuate them, as he moved from end to end at slip, "by letting the batsmen know an atrocity or two about their parentage". But, for the most part, there seethed a contemplative *hauteur*.

Lillee and Marsh were always, at least less sinister, more extrovert, about their Pommie-bashing. On the whole they were carefree confident that their deeds would outweigh their devilry. You dared ask for their autograph. Actually, one fancies that the two of them—at 36, Marsh is 18 months older—learned their first rudiments in aggro, not from the gangland boss, Ian Chappell, but from the captain who first picked them for the Western Australia State side, Tony Lock, the spiky, competitive emigré to Perth who used to bowl for Surrey and England with Jim Laker. Lock was not even afraid to pooh-pooh the chivalries of public school cricket within earshot of Peter May.

Lillee's longtime nickname was "F.O.T." Only dear friends dare call him so. It recalls the day, as a stringy colt in his first State season, that he was daydreaming in the deep, picking his nose at deep fine-leg. Bellowed the infuriated skipper, Lock, from short-leg—"C'mon, wake up, Lill! Yer an *Effin'Ol'Tart!*"

Marsh, incidentally, answers to the name "Bacchus" not because, as he once did, he beat the hitherto unbeatable Douggie Walters in a marathon lager drinking contest—did I hear 36 cans of Swan on a flight from London?—but because there is a place in Australia called Bacchus Marsh. Actually, "Romney" might have been slightly more original.

Together, F.O.T. and Bacchus have been involved in a few tawdry episodes. They each egg the other on, just as they do when they are concentrating only on the cricket. A few years ago, in Perth, Lillee went out to bat against England with one of his sponsor's experimental aluminium bats. When the England captain, Brearley, objected that it would ruin the ball, Lillee said he was quite prepared to leave the advertising gimmick at that—till Marsh, batting at the other end, insisted that he was quite within his rights to stay. The spoiled schoolboy's sit-down strike lasted fully ten minutes.

Neither of them admits who first came up with the idea to bet *against* their own team at Headingley a couple of years ago. The bookie says it was Lillee. In the last innings, Australia needed only 130 to win at a doddle. Marsh and Lillee secured odds of 500–1 that England would be victorious. England won. Lillee collected £5,000, Marsh £2,500. "There was no question of us not trying to win the game for Australia", insists Lillee—and with 17 runs he was the third top scorer. But, for many cricket lovers in Australia, the stench remains.

Even Marsh, however, thinks Lillee went too far the following winter when he spitefully kicked the Pakistan captain, Javed Miandad, at the wicket. One day, says Marsh, even Dennis will admit that was wrong. Lillee meanwhile sticks to his original story—"It wasn't a kick; I just tapped his rump with my boot."

The following season, against New Zealand, the crucial match reached a marvellously dramatic climax. There was one ball left and New Zealand needed just one sixer to win. Greg Chappell shamefully ordered his bowler to bowl an underarm daisy-cutter all along the ground. It was impossible to hit. The captain's long suspected meanness of spirit was at last fully revealed.

And yet, the great multitude of cricketers enjoy their game when—indeed, because—it is noble and generous and forgiving. Foes must be honoured. And the younger Chappell, at the wicket, had a poise and grace and grandeur when he drove through mid-off that had been seldom matched in the long litany of lore. Alas, in a way, but his talent *did* outshine the poverty of his sportsmanship. And as Chappell stood there in the field, glowering grim at slip, next to him would be Marsh, gloved and padded, bouncy, bristling with belligerence and buried in his green cap... and, far away, the macho man, Lillee, would lick his right index finger as he turned on his mark; a preliminary stutter into his stride; then the momentum would gather, and so would the gale that billowed the back of his shirt, and so would the noise from the baying throng; now, as the gold chain whirled and glinted, the stride would lengthen, and the batsman would swallow, scared; the cocked grenade would be primed as it pumped away under Lillee's chin; the crowd's tattoo would reach crescendo as, in a feverish jingle-jangle of arms and elbows and legs, out would come the pin in a whirr and a stretch and a grunt...

Then Chappell, deadpan at slip, would unbend, Marsh, in the gloves, would return the ball with a smug, sadist's grin, and Lillee would set off back to his mark...

Three very missable men, who will very much be missed.

"I think he comes from the English side of the family."

The Red Sausage-roll

A.P. HERBERT

January 27 1926

"GEORGE," I shouted as the train rushed out of the tunnel, "in my opinion the Government of Queensland is a Bolshie, Socialist and utterly reprehensible Government, George, but, by George, George, their sausage-rolls are bonzer!"

"Good-o!" shouted George, waving his glass and clinging to the rocking table. "Haddock, old man," shouted George, "the principles of this Government are detestable—I say, their principles are unsym—are unsympathetic"—George here for a long while gazed vaguely through the window at the flying night—"but, by Haddock, Haddock," he continued at last, "their hospitality is dinkum!"

It was long after midnight. The reason the table was rocking, the reason the night was flying, the reason we were all shouting was simply this: that we were in a train, an admirable special train provided by the Labour Government of Queensland, but roaring terribly through the night along the terrible permanent-way of the Queensland Railway, which is three feet six inches wide. For my part I was too frightened to go to bed; for it seemed impossible that that bouncing, banging, rolling, roaring, volatile train could live through the night. And the rest of the Mission were too busy cementing the Empire and exchanging lies. So there we sat in the long saloon—Canadians, New Zealanders, South Africans, Australians, Welshmen, Englishmen, and one brave gentleman from Malta—shouting across the little tables and bit by bit putting the Empire straight. Canadians told the Australians what they thought about their politics; Welshmen in a few brief words re-organised their industries; and Englishmen with a sweep of the hand settled, populated and developed the entire Commonwealth. While the Australians, when they could insinuate a word, indicated in a terse phrase or two the way in which Great Britain's manufactories, finance and commerce would be best conducted. And not a head broken, not a cross look!

And all the time in unbroken Imperial unity we ate deep, deep, the Socialist sausage-roll and drank the health of Australia in the generous cups provided by the vile Government of Queensland. There were in that saloon direct representatives of that Government, a Government, Sir, which has destroyed the Second Chamber and established State fish-shops; there were in that saloon minions of the Government in the service of the Railway Department, a Department, Sir, which notoriously runs these foully-nationalised railways at a loss for the benefit of the railway-workers. Yet, as George, proud Tory, raised to his lips his seventh glass of Socialist champagne, he never blenched. On the contrary, I distinctly saw him drink the health of a Railway Commissioner in the pay of men who had abolished a Second Chamber—*pop*!

But Honeybubble was of finer clay. Honeybubble had just been hearing the full and horrible tale of a recent Queensland railway strike, and he was all worked up.

"Mr Honeybubble—a sausage-roll?" cried George, hospitably waving a plateful at him.

"No, boy," said Honeybubble, and with a grand gesture he waved the tainted food away. But, the train just then giving a violent lurch to starboard, two rolls fell flying from the plate, and Honeybubble struck one of them with his hand so that it flew like a tennis-ball across the train into the lap of a Canadian editor, who eagerly devoured it. Such is night-life in our great Dominion.

"In my opinion, boy," continued Honeybubble, undaunted, and leaning forward and speaking very clearly and earnestly, "all this—this *refreshment* is no more than a *bribe*."

"A *what*, Mr Honeybubble?" shouted George, speaking not quite so clearly.

"A *bribe*, boy—a BRIBE!" shrieked Honeybubble against the maddening clatter of the train. "They are afraid," he went on intensely, "*that we shall go back to England and tell the truth!* A bribe, boy."

"Mr Honeybubble," said George gravely but indistinctly, "I have no doubt that what you say is correct, and for my part," he said, brandishing the unconsumed portion of a sausage-roll, "I propose to accept the bribe in the spirit in which it is offered. Steward," he said, to a passing Socialist, "bring these gentlemen two large bribes-and-sodas!"

The intelligent Australian instantly took his meaning and withdrew.

"Do you know," went on Honeybubble, more and more intense, "that in the recent railway strike *they picketed the roads?*"

"Revolting," said George.

"Do you know that for eight days not a wheel moved, not a letter was delivered, and the Government lifted not a finger to protect the community?"

"Intolerable," said George.

"Do you know," said Honeybubble, warming up, "that at the end of it the Government surrendered everything—with the exception of the thirty-six and three-quarter hour week for clerical workers?"

"Hideous," said George.

"Do you know that the employees of this very railway assert their right to hold 'stop-work' meetings during working-hours and that this 'right' has been practically conceded?"

"Frightful," said George.

"By a Labour Government drawing large salaries and afraid of their own supporters?"

"*Too* awful," said George.

"And yet you sit there eating and drinking at their expense," concluded Honeybubble powerfully.

"Disgusting," said George with his eyes closed.

"Do you realise, boy, that at any moment they might stop this train to hold a political meeting?"

"They mustn't take the sausage-rolls," said George good-humouredly, "and they mustn't close the bar. But if that is understood the sooner this rackety train stops the better. Steward," he said to the genial attendant, "in case you feel like a stop-work meeting during the night we'd better have some more tongue sandwiches, and if you don't bring some more champagne I shall tell everybody about the Queensland Government."

"Good-o," said the steward, beaming.

"Good-o, as you say," said George, rising and swaying slightly: perhaps it was the train. "And now, Mr Honeybubble, having sold my soul for the flesh-pots, I shall follow the thing to its logical conclusion and I shall sing a Bolshie song. For in my opinion the Socialists of Queensland are not merely dinkum, Mr Honeybubble, but bonzer, Mr Honeybubble, and I shall therefore sing 'Parasite in this Fair Country.' I should be glad, gentlemen," said George, leaning against the table, "if the Canadian delegates would stop singing 'O Canada!' if only for a minute, and join with me in singing 'Parasites in this Fair Country.' Page forty-four. Gentlemen, the forty-fourth page in the Scarlet Song-Book of the Industrial Workers of the World (Third Australian Edition).

George had drawn from his pocket the horrible red book referred to (purchased illicitly on a Sunday afternoon on the "Domain" at Sydney), and, swaying still but no longer slightly, he sang the following remarkable words to the fair and ancient tune of "Annie Laurie", as indicated in the book:—

THE PARASITES

By JOHN E. NORDQUIST.

(*Tune: "Annie Laurie."*)

Parasites in this fair country live on
honest labour's sweat;
There are some who never labour, yet
labour's product get;
They never starve or freeze, nor face the
wintry breeze,
They are well fed, clothed and sheltered,
And they do what'er they please.

These parasites would vanish and leave
this grand old world
If the workers fought together and the
workers' flag unfurled;
When in One Union grand the working-
class shall stand
The parasites will vanish,
And the workers rule the land.

Any reader who is familiar with that grand old air I recommend to sing to it here and now these grand new words, and then picture to himself that midnight scene, where, against the clatter and roar of the train, the sons of Empire, called together from the four corners of the world, bellowed into the bush that noble twentieth-century hymn. After it we sang (to the tune of "Redwing"):

Shall we still be slaves and work for
wages?
It is outrageous,
Has been for ages...

And after that (to "John Brown's Body") the soul-stirring chorus—

Solidarity for ever!
Solidarity for ever!
Solidarity for ever!
In the One Big U-ni-ion!

After that we took another bribe or two and reorganised the Empire for the last time. Then we went to bed. And, though we had travelled in a mob for many months, many thousands of miles, and argued incessantly; though there was not one single subject upon which more than two of us agreed; yet we reeled along the rolling, shattering corridor, one heart, one mind, one voice, singing "Solidarity for ever!" and sometimes arm-in-arm. And what I say is that an Empire in which such things can happen has just a little life in it yet.

Meanwhile Honeybubble had furtively consumed the last sausage-roll.

Australian Report

In 1974, Joan Bakewell visited the land which has been giving the Poms such a hard time. This is the report she sent us.

I MADE my preparations to the extent of 20 lbs. excess luggage—but I still was not prepared for Australia. I assiduously stashed away toothpaste, plasters, T.C.P., shampoo, face cream, Kleenex and the heavier armoury of hair dryer, rollers and travelling iron, for all the world as though I anticipated some Hepburn-style safari in the steps of Burke and Wills. In some unconscious corner of my mind's eye, I think I saw myself outfacing the outback with impeccably varnished nails and no split ends. It was not to be. I landed in one of the world's highest-speed consumer societies, positively groaning under the load of its own Kleenex, toothpaste, hair-rollers: exploding with affluence and driving one to chipped nails and split ends in an effort to utilise all its civilising commodities at once.

Even those barren plains, those dusty hills are a front. Below their surface heaves the great untapped: an abundance of coal, lead, iron, oil and tin that with one deft flick of the economy will one day have Australia thumbing its nose at the rest of the impoverished world. Around her coasts the seas abound in fish. Nothing so undignified as our current scrabble for North Sea scraps. Here you can come away from the fish and chip shop with 30 cents of chips and a dollar's worth of great white killer underneath the salt and vinegar.

Australia thinks big. It gives them a jaunty confidence. Each day their press claims a new world-beater. "Australia leads the world" runs the familiar headline: beneath the message continues—"in price rises". I had expected to be benignly patronising, sipping a sunset gin on some colonial balcony and asking after the Aborigines. Instead I arrived to find Britain the subject of their pity and the government's Advisor on Aboriginal Affairs quite able to fend for himself without my liberal concern—stirring up a brew of trouble that kept him in the headlines for nigh on two weeks.

I thought I was prepared for the people too. I'd boned up on Barry Mackenzie and reckoned the occasional "Jeez, mate" dropped into the conversation would give me a sense of belonging—rather as "Alors, eh bien . . . " does in France. No such bogus fraternising of course ever disguises one's transparent Englishness. And Australians are wise to it. Ever since the first convicts were prancing round supposedly with Prisoner of His Majesty writ across their vests, the Aussies have been very wary of the POHMs. Alternative versions give Pom as derived from pomegranate—typifying the English complexion (whatever happened to peaches and cream?) But in either case it has nothing to do with the highest praise a Bazza can pay his girl: "She's apples". So the cut glass accent is a distinct hazard—and the imperial tones that once rang across Harrods cut no ice in the Botany Bay deli. Fortunately, at a time when

New Zealand was running its "Punch a Pom a day" campaign, the Northern inflection in my voice rang a few bells. "I've a brother in Didbury", "I come from Blackpool", "I was born in Prestwich". It seemed days before we met our first actual native born Australian. The hotelier was Greek, chamber maid Polish, the waitress came from Germany. And we think we've got immigrants! OK—without ours the National Health would collapse. Without theirs, Australia would close down.

I did sometimes feel that Barry Humphries invented Australia: and now they can't forgive him for it. Worthy public figures are constantly decrying the "Bazza" image, while their colleagues go off to beer and prawn parties that bring down the government. Qantas is even now making a promotional film aimed at breaking down the rough uncultured image of Australia usually associated with Chips Rafferty. When I was 13 I was in love with Chips Rafferty who was too busy herding his cattle (or was it sheep?) across the deserts of Australia to notice the pigtailed schoolgirl in the stalls. To stamp out that image is to trample all over my dreams. Better by far to cash in on our well-rooted prejudices and cash in on the wild colonial boy. How about letting rip with "Bazza is beautiful" and "bring back the Bazza" as a campaign to put the grit back into a nation at risk of going soft on surf riding and lying in the sun. That indeed is how I met my own "Bazza". I was lying alone on what I supposed was an empty beach (after all, the temperature had dropped to the 80s—by Australian standards a cold snap) trying to keep the sand out of my nostrils and my mind on Patrick White. He loomed up from nowhere, gave my pasty English skin a contemptuous going over and sat down to chat. "Here we go", I thought, "the Australian chat-up." He was the colour of Worcester sauce, had shaggy shorts and a shapeless towelling hat which he kept on. "Yes, I'm on holiday"—we both were. "No, I didn't know Adelaide well"—neither of us did. "Yes, from England"—no response. The minutes groaned by between exchanges: the Patrick White lay half buried in drifting sand. Then I sensed him move in for the kill. "This is it", I thought, "'No' is the same in any continent." "Tell me," he edged nearer, the tone muted with feeling, "what are the life-saving clubs really like on the south coast of England?"

However obtuse the personal preoccupations of the men, the Australian women appear bound together by one common interest. Witness a typical passage from the social coverage of Adelaide's Festival of the Arts:

> "Sir Roland and Lady Jacobs—pearl embroidery highlighted her slim deep pink dress, Festival trustee (Mr J. V. S. Bowen) and Mrs Bowen, her slim ice blue dress was encrusted with crystals at the neckline, were in the audience."

Clothes, it seems, take precedence even over grammar. Detailed accounts of frills and lace, drapery and embroidery fill column inches a critic might envy. The gay parade of social life stares out daily from the blurred newsprint as people's attendance is noted in terms of hand-printed silk, flame chiffon and multi-coloured beading. Men defined by job and position: women by their wardrobe. It's not hard to see where Germaine Greer got the fire in her belly.

Finally, I expected to find Australia puritanical: the frontier country that takes offence at the decadent ruderies of Alf Garnett and Peter Cook. Those days it seems are over. In fact I found porno newspapers spilling over newsagents counters everywhere I went. On the principle—know a country, know its porn—I cautiously purchased a copy of each. The man ahead of me—sun-bronzed, shaggy shorts, towel hat, a real Bazza—bought six of each. Perhaps he was going to paper the wall with them. Perhaps his wife wore hand-embroidered satin with pearls at the neckline.

At the other extreme Australia's Mary Whitehouse, a certain Mrs Van D. Brown has taken her stand somewhere to the right of Queen Victoria, declaring *The Forsyte Saga* to be little but filth from first to last. She, at least, I hope kept a straight face when the government slapped an entertainment tax on the pill. Some country!

Aussie Acting

SHERIDAN MORLEY

Sydney

I AM not, I fear, very Australian. My brother, ten years younger, thinner, sexier and resident here this past decade with a mahogany tan to prove it, reckons this is because I lack the secret of youth. I, on the other hand, incline to the view that Australia is actually too old for me rather than I for it, and take consolation from the fact that seventy-five percent of local Sydney schoolchildren, asked what they would most like to be in life, said retired. There is not, so far as I can make out, a lot going on here. True, there is my father, giving what I would tell you, were I not his son, is the most marvellously touching and bittersweet portrayal of the reluctantly homebound spy eking out the last days of a Russian exile in Alan Bennett's *The Old Country*, a production in which Wallas Eaton (he who was once our very own Wealthy Wal in *Take It From Here*) is also infinitely more jokey and moving than the original London casting of the role. But beyond that, what? Well, in the thirty-one years since I was last here, when the going rate for a child actor (which I occasionally was) ran to two shillings per matinee, they have of course built the Sydney Opera House, a flamboyantly if irrelevantly winged structure which rises out of the harbour like a baroque National Car Park, and under whose wings there is now a new theatre where Frank Thring, known locally as the Thring from Outer Space, is playing the Michael Redgrave role in Simon Gray's *Close of Play*. This too seems to have improved on its journey to the other side of the world: both plays were in London treated by actors and directors alike with a kind of desiccated respect, and there

isn't too much time for that sort of thing down here, where the dramatic priorities appear to be getting on with the jokes and trying to make sure that the customers understand the plot, or at least enough of it to get down the final curtain. I do not wish to suggest that Australians are not natural theatregoers, merely that they look curiously relieved once on their way back to their cars.

This must be the only nation in the world where seven is a winning score on *Mastermind* and where telecommercials exhort us to THINK AUSTRALIA. I keep thinking of the 24-hour plane journey out here, which resembled nothing so much as a Darby and Joan airborne outing that all the Darbys had somehow missed: they even played Bobby Howes on the headphones. "What do you think of Australia?" a brave journalist once asked my father, who as it happens has always loved it; "What does it matter what I think of it?" replied Robert, "You're the one who has to live here." But they do seem to like to know what we think, and what I think is that the best thing about Sydney is the Nimrod. Situated in what appears to be a disused air-raid shelter near a shop calling itself the Depilatory Capital of New South Wales, this is a theatre complex which has already given the world *The Elocution of Benjamin Franklin* and much of the best of David Williamson, including his *The Club* which is still to be found at the Old Vic. But the surprising thing about *Traitors* is first that it's not in fact yet another Williamson, and second that it's the work of a young Brisbane writer with only one other play to his name. This one is set in

Leningrad and Moscow in 1927 and tells simply, if often brutally and bloodily, the story of the collapse of the Russian Revolution.

Ten years on from the dreams and ideals of 1917, communism has disintegrated into a savage internal struggle between Stalin's thugs and the last of the Trotsky idealists and around that theme of disillusion and death Stephen Sewell has woven an admittedly overlong three-hour drama of immense raw vitality. The message of the play is that communism, like capitalism, was built out of the blood of the workers, and though this may place Sewell politically some way to the right of Barker, Brenton and Hare his writing has many of their strengths. Nimrod has recently been through considerable internal troubles of its own, but this production by their new artistic director Neil Armfield promises well for the future and needs to be seen soon in London: Michele Fawdon and Barry Otto lead a grittily good cast.

Over on the other side of town, just near where a shop is selling packets of wine dust (not a ready mix, you understand, but for sprinkling over your bottles to make them look as though they've been in a cellar and not the local supermarket) Mollie Sugden from *Are You Being Served?* is to be found in a ramshackle farce, soon to be followed by John Inman in one even more ramshackle. Once you've got a hit tele-series out here, the thing to do is apparently make a dash for the theatre and clean up before the customers forget or move on to another series. English actors appearing here ought to be made to sign a declaration that the show they are playing is one they would be willing to have the West End see them in.

But the Australian theatre is even more perilous than most: my brother, who is a producer here (a job not unlike running a car-wash concession in the desert) found himself the other night talking to a fellow theatregoer in the interval after the first act of Derek Jacobi's visiting *Hamlet* "Bloody long," said the Sydney man; "Yes," agreed my brother, "the first act of *Hamlet* has been that long for about four hundred years." "Then you'd think," said the Sydney man, "that by now they'd have done something about it."

Christmas Down Under

by HONEYSETT

"Don't you know any football songs?"

"*And mother says you're not to practise on the cat.*"

"***You'd think he could try and be a bit more original for a change.***"

IN STRICT TRAINING.

YOUNG ENGLAND. "PLEASE, SIR, MAY I HAVE YOUR AUTOGRAPH?"
AUSTRALIA. "SORRY, BUT I'M NOT ALLOWED TO WRITE ANYTHING ON THIS TOUR."
YOUNG ENGLAND. "NOT EVEN A RECEIPT FOR THE ASHES?"

The Hash England Made of the Ashes

COMPTON MACKENZIE

It is not often that England win the Ashes—but back in 1955 they did. Although, as Compton Mackenzie reported for Punch *at the time, this was not one of the great Len Hutton's best performances.*

THE somersaults turned by cricket correspondents after the Test Match at Adelaide have prompted our own carping correspondent to deflate the English team before they start the final Test at Sydney:

Yes, England has won the Ashes, but like almost every other cricket expert sent out by the press to Australia I consider that everything Hutton did was wrong. I feel so strongly about this that I cannot bring myself to call him Len. What right had he to lose the toss at Adelaide? Surely Hutton has been playing cricket long enough to know that the first duty of a captain is to win the toss. He should have had a double-headed coin and a double-tailed coin; anybody with as many strokes at his service as Hutton should possess enough sleight of hand to use them effectively. The argument that such a trick would not be cricket is out of date. Cricket is not cricket today except when the authors and the publishers dabble about in the rain at Vincent Square. And even if cricket were still cricket a Test Match would not be cricket. A Test Match is something between trench warfare, mounting a bus in the rush hour, and waiting for a train on British Railways on the evening of Bank Holiday.

Hutton has had two first-class fast bowlers, but he has used them as if they were playing a game. When one remembers what Jardine could do with the body-line bowling of Larwood, it was surely not too much to expect that Hutton with Tyson and Statham at his disposal would have made sure that not a single member of the Australian eleven left the field alive. The excuse that the weather was too hot on the first day to think what anybody ought to do next will not stand examination. Noël Coward once made it perfectly clear to the rest of the world that mad dogs and Englishmen enjoy rushing about in the sun. Yes, but England won the fourth Test. I prefer to say that Australia lost it, which is not the same thing. If Australia had won should we not all agree that England lost?

Hutton made a big mistake before he muffed the toss by not playing Bedser. The fact that England won without Bedser is no answer. It was a grave error of judgment not to play Bedser, as most of the armchair critics at once pointed out. It is not fair to sneer at armchair critics. They are in a much better position to judge what ought to be done than men playing in a temperature of 110°. They see the struggle as a whole and can cable home to their papers an objective view of it.

Why did Hutton tell Cowdrey to use his nose to stop a ball at short-leg? Cowdrey is a stocky young man but he is not an elephant, and a cricket ball is much harder than even the buns at the Zoo. Cowdrey may own the auspicious initials M.C.C., but that does not mean he can perform the impossible. Would Hutton ask the Mayor of Pudsey to field with his nose?

Then there was that six when Wardle hit the ball at a lady among the spectators who had to receive first-aid from the ambulance men. If Wardle wanted to hit a six why did not Hutton tell him to aim at the press box? Your

"Back in England they'll be still in bed . . .

. . . fast asleep, dreaming of the Test and a fighting backs-to-the-wall display.

'Baverley's Great Innings. Invaluable'. Yes, it's

. . . up to me. The openers have failed and we've no tail to speak of.

carping correspondent and every other carping correspondent, like London, could have taken it.

Dickens' Mr Wardle would never have behaved like that. Even if his sister had been sitting among the spectators at Muggleton with Alfred Jingle's arm round her waist, Mr Wardle would never have tried to hit her with a cricket ball. The only conceivable occasion on which one could forgive Wardle for such unchivalrous behaviour would be if he heard George Formby singing "My luve is like a red, red rose" to a female spectator at Old Trafford when Lancashire were winning.

Whatever Hutton did he was wrong. After he was out at 80, when any moderately good captain would have hit a century, he apparently told Compton and Cowdrey not to make any runs at all for two hours. That is not

I mustn't let 'em down. I can't.

In Fleet Street they'll be taking down every run. I can see the headlines . . .

'Baverley to the Rescue' . . .

In another hour they'll be waking up, switching on, and saying 'Thank goodness we've still got . . .'"

"Ah, Saturday again and good old soccer."

the way to win even a Test Match. Yes of course I know that England won. But why did Hutton allow the kangaroo to wag its tail by putting on something like a hundred runs for the eighth wicket? Hutton may argue that the tail of the kangaroo is a much more efficient organ than the kinked tail of a bulldog, but that only goes to show that he should have played Bedser and Loader. In justice to Hutton it must be pointed out that the M.C.C. selectors picked the wrong team to send out to Australia, as was only too painfully apparent at Brisbane. Another mistake Hutton made was in letting some of his team off to go and watch the Davis Cup tennis matches between Australia and the United States. Any one of them might easily have cricked his neck, and nobody can play good cricket with a cricked neck. Fortunately no harm was done, but Hutton took a serious risk in allowing his players time off to watch tennis.

However, in spite of all that Hutton and the touring side did to prevent it, England has the Ashes, and your carping correspondent can only wish that the ash-bin in which they rest were not quite so badly dented. Yes, England has won the rubber, but I hope people at home realise how much they owe to the cricket correspondents whose cool, confident, friendly and always infallible advice has made Hutton's task a sinecure.

****

1852

GOLDEN DREAMS

To some minds, perhaps, the golden legends which constitute the news from Australia may be interesting; but it is probable that the discovery of the precious metal at the Antipodes will lead to a diminution of interest. Indeed, it is to be apprehended that gold will cease to be precious in quality, and be precious only in quantity, to such an extent that a number of sovereigns will no longer be capable of being considered tantamount to so much tin. It will be necessary to make jewels the media of exchange; and then we shall be sending for change for a diamond, which will be given in emeralds and rubies. A metallic substitute for gold might be found in platinum, which is scarce; the only objection to it is that the word has no legitimate rhyme, and would be unsuited for the use of poets, or rather for their abuse: for most of them decry and villify gold, although, like other people, they are glad to get as much of it as they can.

****

Out Down Under

ROBERT MORLEY

ON wet afternoons in Cheltenham when I was rather younger I would borrow a pudding basin from the cook, half fill it with water, place a Swan Vestas on the surface and inscribe a card announcing FLOATING MATCH. TO VIEW ONE PENNY. Reluctantly my parents would occasionally oblige with a coin but seldom my sister.

"We've had it, Bobby," she used to tell me. I have had all my life a fatal tendency to stretch the joke.

I bethought me of Cheltenham when I finally reached the Bimini Wild Life Park after a desperate search among the Dandenongs, a range of hills beyond Melbourne where every other house is a restaurant bearing the message, mysterious to the uninitiated, "B.Y.O.", which means bring your own Fosters or whatever, or drink lemonade.

The Bimini Wild Life Park is signposted from all directions but we kept missing the turning which led into the Reserve itself until finally locating a rough cart track which ended abruptly in front of a small bungalow, the front sitting-room of which sported a soft drink dispenser and a more than ordinarily enraged cockatoo.

It is only fair that we reporters should sometimes go ahead of our readers to spy out the land; indeed, it is our duty and privilege to do so in the case of civil strife and major catastrophe. The Bimini Wild Life Park must surely come under the latter heading.

Half a dozen sun-blackened fields are loosely divided from each other by sagging wires, presumably lest the chickens housed in one paddock should do battle with the hamsters segregated in another. There was a pond with frogs and a hutch with several rabbits. The centre piece of this macabre collection was a display of abandoned motorcar tyres and spare parts in which a kangaroo, a wallaby and a peacock foraged dejectedly. Some effort had been made here to recreate the natural habitat of the marsupials at least, but it was not enough, surely. I was tempted to demand the return of the gate money and then remembered the pudding basin.

"Live and let live" is my motto, which is one of the reasons why I thought it prudent to leave Melbourne before the duck shooting began in earnest.

For some time the television and press have carried warnings of the impending danger. Australians are famous for getting their heads shot off during the mad month of March, or drowning in icy water while attempting to retrieve their retrievers similarly employed with a dead bird.

One of the more mysterious television programmes put out by Government sources here recently is an educational film showing a would-be hunter in the act of "Dialling a Duck". The telephone appears to be growing in the bullrushes, and anyone can pick it up and enquire of the answering service in which direction the birds are currently flying. My local *Tasman Mercury* reports that at least two were killed (humans, not ducks) on the first day and another had his eye shot out by a friend whose own wasn't in as yet. As for the ducks, they take temporary refuge in the local parks and Botanical Gardens.

Ninety per cent of the tourists who come to Hobart go to Port Arthur as soon as they arrive. The other great attraction being the Casino, the only one in Australia to date, although plans are on foot to open another in Darwin which badly needs an aid to survival as a tourist trap after the disastrous earthquake, or was it a cyclone—how short is memory, alas.

The memory of the tragedy which overtook Hobart in '76 is still fresh, however. Almost exactly five years ago a tanker laden with zinc from the smelting works upstream rammed the bridge which is Hobart's lifeline with its two harbour shores and sank along with eight cars crossing at the time. Only a few bodies were ever recovered, and cars and ship lie on the river bed under the impenetrable silt. It took three years for the bridge to be rebuilt, along with the courage of the citizens who live on the further shore.

Port Arthur, however, is safely behind them and is now a National Park, preserving (as far as possible after demolition and two disastrous fires) its grim history of sado-masochism as it was practised for 30 years during the latter part of last century when the Penal Settlement there took root, blossomed and finally—and much to the annoyance of those who employed cheap labour thereabouts—expired.

It's a small world but somehow I didn't expect to find Tony Armstrong-Jones already *in situ* snapping the Model Prison, as the block devoted to solitary confinement used to be called. Prisoners were kept in silence and darkness, being forced to wear a visor over the face when visiting divine service and, when passing each other in the corridors, to proceed back to back. Nowadays visitors are treated to a film reproducing conditions under which the settlement operated and small children clap with glee when shown pictures, admittedly largely imaginary, of dogs who were kept chained and ravenous a few inches apart and housed in barrels to prevent escapes across the neck of the Peninsula on which the colony was sighted.

There was also a train running from the nearest town and powered by convicts to convey VIPs on tours of inspection. The track ran up and down dale for a distance of eight miles and the only concession made to the unfortunate handlers was permission to ride downhill if not too exhausted to climb aboard.

Juvenile offenders, who from the age of nine could be deported from Britain for stealing a pheasant, or even a book, were housed separately and taught a trade at which, when they had become proficient, they were expected to earn their living, and were indentured to an Apprentice Master and, curious to relate, often subsequently prospered and started businesses of their own throughout the colony.

The cheerful Guide recounted fearful tales of bands of convicts who did escape, and how often the smallest ones were eaten by their companions and the survivors took to bush-ranging with considerable success. Quite how they avoided the dogs was never explained, but studying the pictures afterwards I decided a quick leap over the barrels would have been just feasible, supposing myself to be in better condition than I am today and that the guards who were supposed to be patrolling at the time were otherwise engaged. Swimming was out of the question—it seems that the sharks in those days were as hungry as everyone else.

It started to rain and I sought shelter in the lunatic asylum, only recently shut down, apparently. But then I suppose by now there are too many of us at $2.00 a time. In the evening I sought solace at the roulette table in company with a fellow from the *Guardian* still keeping his readers in touch with the cricket scene, which seems to have mercifully faded.

Brisbane, or rather Surfers' Paradise, where we are currently holed up, is not quite the sundrenched playground I was expecting. The winds which lash the surf also bring heavy cloud banks and tropical downpours and the coastline is somewhat marred with skyscrapers in all stages of development and decorated with enormous banners indicating that whatever else awaits completion, the letting office is open for business.

Here, as in Brisbane itself, the special delicacy in the eateries are mud crab and Brisbane bugs, a delectable crayfish. There are miles and miles of sand, some intrepid surfers and, it must be confessed, a goodly number of bathing fatalities due to the dangerous and seemingly ever-present rip tides.

Across the lagoon from our condominium is the home of the late Gladys Montcrieff who reigned supreme on the Australian musical comedy stage for fifty years and appeared for five of them in *The Maid of the Mountains*. In those bygone days, plays seemed to manage to survive longer than the fortnight that is now a more usual period for a visiting company. What, you may ask, has happened to the theatre and what to Gladys? The latter question's more easily answered; she died and was buried and visitors passing her home on excursion boats still buy roses and gladioli and attempt to hurl them onto the lawn which comes down to the water edge, just as Gladys was wont to do if the boat was sufficiently full, and her friend and companion for many years, Elsie Wilson, continues to do this every day.

There is loyalty for you and, catching a little of the mood, I myself opened the latest memorial to her, a bar hung with old photographs of the star and a restaurant in which every dish is named after one of her triumphs. We had Crab Salad Iolanthe, Veal Blue Mazurka, Mousse Chocolate Soldier and Coffee Merry Widow. Melba, who had to content herself with toast and icecream, once heard Miss Moncrieff at an audition when she was unwise enough to attempt one of the Diva's own arias and firmly advised her to stick to musical comedy.

Later, when they met again at a Charity Concert, she was reported to have reprimanded our Gladys for mispronunciation. The word, she told her is "love, dear, with an O, not a U". Melba, they say, was rather devoid of human affection, but Gladys Moncrieff was LUV to all who knew her and to a great many of those who did not.

To travel North is the dream of many Australians who find life in Sydney, Melbourne and even Brisbane passing too quickly in a dull round of surburban routine. They dream of the day when with the toilet training, the school run, the part-time job behind the counter of the fast food kiosk or the bar of the local finished, they can uproot sticks and their old man and move on to pastures new—a small banana plantation or a pineapple farm in the rain forest beyond Cairns. Luckily perhaps for most, it must remain a dream, but some are valiant enough to reach the Northern Tip of Queensland where the road ends abruptly; there they grow sugar cane, construct fish traps and scratch some sort of a living tending the occasional paw-paw. It is not a particularly easy life but then life is no longer as easy as it was in any part of this once happy-go-lucky country, where unions and government wrestle for power and they say the Prime Minister sleeps with a photograph of Mrs Thatcher under his pillow; or it could just possibly be the other way round.

AUSTRALIAN CULTURE TAKES OVER

This year's Reith Lecture given by LORD JAMES OF CIVILISATION (with some help from Miles Kington)

HELLO THERE. This year's Reith Lecture is on the subject of Australian culture, though some people might say that the two things are a contradiction of terms. Well, some people will say anything for money. Take me for example; at the moment I'm very busy writing a play, a TV column, a book of essays and the longest poem in the world—and that's just with my *left* hand, so you can see that I'm right up to here in work and I shouldn't be doing this lecture at all, but what the hell, you get reprint fees in the *Listener* and I gather the BBC have almost succeeded in selling the programme to Radio Fiji, so I'm very grateful to Miles Kington for writing this lecture for me.

Where was I? Oh yeah, Australian culture. It may come as a surprise to you to learn that I am actually an Australian because it's not a thing I go round stressing much. I live in England, I write about an amazing variety of subjects, I travel a lot, I talk a lot, which makes me a cosmopolite if anything. However, the close observer (and believe me, I've never known the *Observer* be so close) as I was saying, the careful spectator (see previous bracket) will have noticed that the one place I don't go to much, or write about, or care to have mentioned in front of me, is Australia.

There is a reason for this.

There are *two* cultures in Australia.

One is vulgar, earthy, cheerful, Philistine, insensitive and chauvinistic. The chief arts associated with this side of the Australian character are tennis, cricket, swimming and throwing cans of Fosters lager. It has also produced jokes against the Pommies as well as Rolf Harris, or rather jokes against the Pommies including Rolf Harris. By these standards the greatest Australian artist of all time is Rigby. (Sorry Rolf.)

The other culture is serious, learned, cultivated, distinguished and international. As such, it is of no interest to the vast majority of Australians, who belong to the first culture. Australian writers and artists receive so little attention in their own country that most of them go abroad to write and paint. A few, like the great novelist Patrick White, stay at home in Australia, but his books are only read abroad. By expatriate Australians. The result is that the Australians belonging to the second culture do not make a great show of their country of origin, except Rolf Harris who of course belongs to the first culture and is a better swimmer than painter.

Let me give you an example of the clash of the two cultures.

Recently the Australian Government

decided they needed a new national anthem instead of the old singalong tunes so far used for knees-up purposes, and organised a competition for which they received thousands of dignified new songs. This was a victory for the second culture.

Having looked at them all, they then decided they might as well stick to the old tunes. This was a victory for the first culture.

Let me give you another example of the culture clash in Australia. For many years we, or at any rate they, have produced some of the best wines in the world. (May I mention in passing Lindeman's Cawarra Hock, a dry, delicate, white wine with crispy overtones?)

But wine has never quite caught on in Australia as it deserves. Because of its mandarin, high-class overtones? Not at all. Because it doesn't come in cans. What's the fun of a Wynn's Coonawarra Estate Hermitage (a tough no-nonsense red) if you can't hurl it at a departing English batsman?

Anyway, as I was saying, never did I like it to be noised abroad that I'm an Australian and I take great pains to avoid Earls Court if I'm ever travelling on the London underground (talking of which, whatever happened to Richard Neville?). But I have recently come to the conclusion that we Australians will never overcome *unless the two cultures combine to form a united front against the decadent pooftah cultural British scene.*

So we have now formed a great two-pronged attack on the soft underbelly of British culture. In the months to come the two cultures of Australia will join forces to

ARRANGEMENT IN GREY AND BLACK (Ma approaching Bondi Beach) Roy Strong's theory that Australia was exerting an influence on art in this country as far back as 1870 was confirmed recently when Whistler's "Portrait of my Mother" was cleaned.

take over the citadel of art in Britain—vulgar and recherché alike will sweep aside all oppositions. Let me name just a few examples.

I. I have been talking to my friend Barry Mackenzie, I mean Barry Humphries, and he has agreed to rewrite the whole of the *Oxford Book of English Verse*. He is especially keen on rewriting Kipling ("Where the dawn comes up like chunder outta China cross the bay...") and Pope ("Alice springs eternal...")

II. I shall be forming an Australian literary XI and touring the country taking on any English eleven that cares to argue against us, thus extending the popularity and dominance of Australian cricket into the cultural field. I have already had T-shirts printed: "... And now the Fastest *Talkers* in the World!"

III. Most of the political cartoonists now working in Britain are from Down Under, (Garland, Jensen, Horner, Gibbard, John Kent etc) and they have agreed to conspire to introduce more Australian-slanted cartoons until by next year few Englishmen will be able to identify the figures in them or indeed understand the captions.

IV. I shall take every opportunity of recommending a better Australian equivalent, if it exists. Fosters has already been established as the premier lager; why not give up champagne and stick to Great West Hermitage Reserve?

V. I have agreed to star in a new Barry Humphries film called "Patrick White Chunders On", the story of an elderly Australian novelist's hilarious escapades in London, and how between booze-ups he manages to diddle the gullible British. The Australian government has agreed to sponsor this film—indeed, many of them wish to appear in it.

VI. As Britain's liberation in the 1960s was entirely in the hands of Australians (Richard Neville, Germaine Greer and others I am too modest to mention), it will be a simple matter to enslave it again, though I cannot reveal our tactics in detail, I can tell you that our first test of strength was to see if we could take over an issue of *Punch*.

Well, must get back to writing the world's longest poem and breaking my own record. Remember, now, always have a bottle of McWilliams Claret handy. Keep a red under your bed.

Sketches of London Wall, Big Ben, St Paul's and Buckingham Palace after completion of restoration and renovation by Sir Richard "Cobber" Seifert. "If Sydney can afford one White Elephant we can afford dozens," says the Minister for the Arts, frequently.

First Steps in Migration

ROY MACGREGOR-HASTIE

During the great British exodus to Australia in the Fifties, Punch *approached Roy MacGregor-Hastie for any words of advice he might have for the migrants.*

ON the assumptions that some fifty per cent of the population of Great Britain will migrate (my assumption), and that 100 per cent of them will go to Australia (their assumption) it is perhaps timely to prepare for the day when you, too, may step ashore at Fremantle and catch your first glimpse of Your New Country.

It will be raining, pattering down melodiously on to the corrugated iron roofs of the wool-sheds on the quayside, turning the last gumtrees from off-white to off-grey, and slowly washing away the incomplete foundations of most of the harbour houses. But you will be heartened at the sight of land; you will be fed up with the food on board, of the ships' officers picking off the best of the women, of the fat man in the bar, of the thin woman on the deck tennis court, of the "comfortable quarters" you have shared with one thousand five hundred others in the tourist third of the ship.

A quartet of immigration officers will be waiting to check your papers before you can get ashore; they will not be wearing uniforms, they will be in old flannel trousers and short-sleeved shirts. They will be called Merv or Bas. All immigration officers are called Merv or Bas; every year a portion of the Merv and Bas crop is set aside for this branch in the future and banished to the Dark Interior to spend twenty years with a tribe. Film units excepted, their return to civilization and taking up of their appointment is the first occasion on which they see white men again, and put aside Magic for Reason, pointing the bone for pointing the finger. They are Angry. You will soon spot this when they thumb through your passport.

You will have spent a summer holiday in Split, perhaps, with a party of students from the National Council of Labour Colleges; your passport will be endorsed with the picturesque visa of Yugoslavia. You may even have taken up residence in Italy, for tax evasion, and that fact will be noted there too. Both these things will distress Merv and Bas. They will discuss their distress:

Merv: Bas!

Bas: Yes, mate, wot you goin' crook about?

Merv: This joker's got this in his passport.

Bas: My flamin' oath. Yoogo-slavvya. I'nt that Commo?

Merv: Too right. You a Commo?

You: No.

Merv: Wot you doin' in Yoogo-slavvya?